Week after week we cycle on,
just doing what we're told.
Until, one day, our life is gone,
and our bodies become cold.

There is no need to live this way,
it's all a state of mind.
Be sure to take some time to play,
and one to another be kind.

So slow down a bit and take your time,
enjoy this life you're given.
Choose for yourself a life sublime,
one that's worth the livin'.

And so my friends I leave you this,
please heed this dire warning.
Live your life a celebration,
and not a life of mourning.

Love Cards

Love is like a turning a card,

it's a game we have to play.

Sometimes easy, sometimes hard,

and sometimes day to day.

When young we flip the first card,

and we end up with a deuce.

Our heart broken to many a shard,

we wonder what's the use?

After a spell the heart does heal,

it's ready to move on.

Sure this time to find the real deal,

but a 5... played like a pawn.

So now, we let a few years go by,

and we find the sweetest date.

Then suddenly we want to die,

when we realize... just an 8.

Now we just want to close the door,

might as well play poker.

But no we'll try it just once more,

and end up with a Joker.

Nope that's it, it's over, we're done,

never again to lose face.

So we refuse to turn another one,

and yet they were the ACE.

Dreams

Whatever happened to your dreams,

The plans for life you'd made?

Long forgotten so it seems,

For monotony you did trade.

Think back for me if you would,

to when you were a child.

Life wasn't based on if you could,

it was just carefree and wild.

Imagination so vivid and free,

for you the sky was the limit.

But they told you to grow up you see,

And their chiding began to dim it.

Then something happened along the way,

and forever you would alter.

A brand new you and much dismay,

And your dreams began to falter.

High school.. College.. and then a job,

Life slowly becoming mundane!

You settled into the workforce mob,

and slowly you went insane.

Now your dreams exist no more,

except maybe in your sleep.

Each day they're left as you close the door,

and work without a peep.

It doesn't have to be this way,

you can change it all you know.

Tomorrow can be a brighter day,

if different seeds you sow.

So reach way back into your mind,

and set your imagination free.

Bring forth your dreams of every kind,

and all possible they will be.

Nowhere

Hurt, battered, and bruised...

Stumbling through the darkness

that has become his life.

Looking for any door or window...

For any sign of light,

but he is denied.

He ponders how he got here,

drowning in this nebulous cloud

of utter darkness...Unable to even see

that which he knows to exist.

His life, at one point, perfection!

The job, woman, and plans,

rapidly coming into motion,

To solidify their hope ..

And their future, just 3 weeks ago!

But then in a moment of weakness,

the man rant...and rant the man did,

from past fear, insecurity, and pain.

Much to the fear of his princess,

So much so that she feared him,

and sent him on his way.

Alone........

Now he wanders aimlessly in the dark,

No light or direction to be found,

Heading only toward three weeks to

Nowhere.

A Loss to Remember

I sit here in the still of night,

listening to the sounds.

whistle of wind, croak of frog,

and the beat as my heart pounds.

My mind begins to wander,

to a different time and place.

A time of wonderful memories,

and Heaven's most beautiful face.

Thing were oh so simple then,

pure and fun and free.

Until something got in the way...

and that something would be me.

I tried so hard to be the one,

who would never cause her pain.

But in the end I hurt her most,

I must have been insane.

So now I sit here in the still of night,

learning how to mend.

For not only did I lose my love,

I lost my true best friend.

Blindness

I lay here in the darkness of night,

the blackness enveloping me

like a death shroud...

I look around the room,

trying to see any speck of light...

any form or figure yet nothing.

I wonder to myself if this

is what it feels like to be blind,

too long to see what one cannot,

to know what exists but never

fathom its form or beauty.

Restlessly I toss and turn,

trying to close my eyes.

longing to drift into sleep...

that peaceful slumber that restores

the body, mind, and soul.

My mind teases me relentlessly...

dangling sleep's sweet slumber

before me, only to rip it away from me

as I reach out to grab it in my embrace...

Replaced by tortuous visions...

Memories of a hauntingly beautiful love,

destroyed from within by a madman...

A man so blinded by his own fears

and his own inadequacies

that he failed to realize hers.

It is then I realize blindness is relative...

And I would choose the other any day....

From Whence I Come

Sitting here in contemplation,

Thoughts running through my brain!

Looking deep within myself,

for answers once again...

Who am I really I ask myself,

And from whence do I come?

You would think I knew the answer,

It really seems quite dumb...

It's really not so simple I say,

to answer quite so quick.

For to tell you just where I come from,

Is truly quite a trick.

The place from whence I come you see,

Is not merely a place.

But a story not so quickly told,

by the furrows on my face.

So just where is this place you ask,

befuddled and confused.

And when no answer quick you get,

You hardly are amused.

This answer that you seek of me,

I will tell you once again.

Is not simply a location,

but a culmination of joy and pain!

For Love

What is this thing we call love,

symbolized by heart or dove?

Tell me something if you please,

is it real or just a tease?

Is love a decision that you choose,

calculated odds of win or lose?

Or is it an emotion that you feel,

betting your all that it is real?

Some say love is spread by Cupid,

others think that totally stupid.

Many believe you simply fall,

and with no choice answer its call.

Sometimes we believe love a curse,

and think there is no feeling worse.

Especially when our heart is broken,

and we think it played like a token.

We hope to find the one someday,

whose love undying lights the way.

One true love that will always last,

and leaves old mistakes in the past.

And if you find that love so true,

be very careful of what you do.

For if you don't it could be toast,

it seems we hurt our loved the most.

Perhaps no greater mystery,

is pondered by both you and me.

There is no doubt that we are smart,

except in matters of the heart.

Apologies

Egregious errors....

Committed unknowingly,

yet shamefully.

How can one do such harm,

yet have no knowledge...

Damage done,

to whom we love most...

Actions devastate,

yet apologies matter not...

for adequate words

are nowhere be found...

in any language...

any diction....

Of the tongue nor the scribe.

The pain caused....

unbearable....

irreversible....

as if time stood still,

and every moment

remembers the anguish...

and they cry, nevermore.

Angel

I stood there among the crowd

as streams of travelers pushed

themselves one past another,

anxious to arrive at their destination.

My heart pounded deep in my chest,

full of excitement and fear so tangible,

as if I could reach out and grab it.

My imagination wandered....

what would I say...

what would I do...

when that long awaited moment arrived.

Minutes seem as an eternity,

as though time has warped upon itself.

Anticipation building, thoughts racing,

pulse bounding out of control...

I feel my knees shaking,

my lips quivering...

the lump in my throat may as well

a boulder be...

Suddenly, in the distance,

I see an aura of light...

Long raven hair put up neatly,

so as to hide the secrets therein.

She draws closer to me,

I glimpse her sparkling eyes...

Her beauty takes my breath away..

my anticipation climaxes.

She wraps her arms around me,

and for a moment time stands still...

And suddenly I realize...

I have touched an angel.

Mother Nature

Who can this lovely maiden be,

in all her splendid glory?

On display for the world to see,

her beauty tells a story.

Her hair by day as glowing sun,

by night a raven black.

A shade of grey she's even done,

when moisture she did lack.

Her clothing lacks in beauty not,

adorned in awesome splendor.

A tapestry that can't be taught,

nor bought from any vendor.

Her spirit can be very sweet,

if she grants you favor.

If so you're in for such a treat,

and her presence you will savor.

But if you dare to cross her,

stay well out of her path.

For soon will come disaster,

from Mother Nature's wrath.

Mine

When, where, who, how...

Questions through my mind race!

Things I long to know right now,

As in this darkness I pace!

The answers they elude me,

haunting even as I ask.

Why God can I not simply see,

from underneath this mask.

Just trust I hear a still voice speak,

and all will be just fine.

Time will reveal the answers you seek,

But until then know you are Mine.

Condemned

Condemned we are,

without them bound

to a past....

A past that damns

our future.....

our hopes.....

our dreams.......

And worst of all.....

Our loves.

Everything

A speck in the mighty cosmos be,

that's all we are- you and me.

In the grand scheme not even dents,

chemically worth a mere 99 cents.

No more than a chemical mix we are,

the same ingredients as earth or star.

So what then makes us so unique?

Pray tell does your curiosity pique?

There is you know just one essence,

which makes distinct our very presence.

Mix those chemicals round in bowl,

Yet nothing we remain 'till added is soul.

Still you wonder what's the use?

Humanity you claim is so obtuse.

You say you're an insignificant being,

But in God's eyes you are everything.

Heaven

I dreamt upon a midnight clear,

a place I wished to be.

A lovely world that knew no fear,

and no one had to flee.

A world without disease or death,

no doctors would we need.

There'd be no thing as one's last breath,

For as spirits we'd be freed.

A world that knows no broken love,

no heartache to be found.

Where one in anger could not shove,

for there does peace abound.

A world without a single crime,

be it theft or murder or rape.

When finally would come a time,

we'd need no hero or cape.

A world that knows no politics,

the power grab is done.

Prestige and money no longer mix,

a greater dominion has won.

It's just a fantasy I hear you say,

no way that it can be.

But I promise you, some day,

that Heaven I will see.

My Love

Where art thou my love?

I know you are there...

hidden amongst the throngs.

Your loveliness beyond my sight,

yet your brilliance such

that blinded is my mind's eye.

I swear I hear your whispers,

carrying softly in the winds...

calling me towards you.

Your voice penetrates my soul,

more powerful than the Sirens of old.

What do you look like my beloved?

Is your hair dark as night?

or flaxen as the sun?

Perhaps it is flaming red,

as the fire within me.

Your eyes....

I cannot even perceive their color,

as you gaze upon me...

consuming my very soul.

The mere cogitation of your touch

renders me languid...

Visions of you haunt my dreams,

and in the day's thoughts

you are ever latent.

Where are you my love?

I know you are there.

how I shall find thee?

Only God knows...

But find thee I will.

Garrett

Grandson how I've watched you grow,
even at times you did not know.
Oftentimes in a forbidden place,
with an impish smile upon your face.

I remember the day that you were born,
and how proudly I was tooting your horn.
I felt as though my heart would burst,
For as my grandson you were the first.

So many memories of many a thing,
amongst the top me pushing your swing.
Up till that day you were deathly afraid,
then, so full of laughter that day as we played.

Now here you are a new sibling and all,
and even so young you step up to the call.
As time passes on I can't wait to see,
the amazing big brother I know you will be.

Best of Show

I see the fear within your eyes,

you know not what to think.

So many trials, hurts, and lies,

you dare not even blink.

You've all but given up on hope,

it's too good to be true.

You feel that you must be a dope,

that something's wrong with you.

You tell me that you don't deserve,

any more than you've got.

Those jerks in the past sure have nerve,

for lies they should be shot.

So look into my eyes and see,

the truth of who you are.

Look deep and see yourself through me,

you'll see a shining star.

A woman with such beauty pure,

it comes from deep inside.

All those who know you can be sure,

in love you do abide.

And let me tell you one more thing,

I think you need to know.

An Angel with a broken wing,

you're still God's "Best of Show".

What Do You See?

When at first you glance upon me,

and spot me with your eyes.

Who is it that you think you see,

and is that truth or lies?

You think that I am bold and brave,

but can't you see my fear?

Or must I take it to my grave,

and never shed a tear?

Perhaps I'm seen aloof and cold,

I never give just take.

But deep inside if truth be told,

my heart's afraid to break.

Maybe I'm just the quiet sort,

without much on my mind.

To that I quickly will retort,

none louder will you find.

Or do you see a gentle soul,

one easy to oppress?

Mistakes like that will take their toll,

with warriors you don't mess.

So now when you glance upon me,

and spot me with your eyes.

Who is it that you think you see,

and is that truth or lies?

Mute

I sit here and I contemplate,

the thoughts within my brain.

So loudly do they resonate,

my head it throbs with pain.

It seems that they are stuck inside,

like there is no way out.

And when I go to speak they hide,

even when I shout.

I know not why they stay in there,

not wanting to be heard.

Some people think I do not care,

if I don't speak a word.

If only they could see the truth,

and look inside my head.

Then I would not appear aloof,

but jovial instead.

So keep in mind this very thought,

if you wish to know 'em.

For this solution I have sought,

to put them in a poem.

Questions

You assume and think you know me,

but you don't have a clue.

There's depths to me you cannot see,

your insights are so few.

To you I don't communicate,

and questions I don't ask.

But how would you annunciate,

a life that long is past.

It's not that I don't wish to know,

what in the past is done.

It's that my past's been hard to hoe,

for me it holds no fun.

So in the past, I do not dwell,

but to the future eye.

In hopes that all someday is well,

and pains of past may die.

So forgive me when I frustrate,

I do not mean to do.

Pray tell I hope it's not too late,

to learn something of you.

For though my past I'd soon forget,

yours is of much import.

Be pain, or joy, or sore regret,

I beg you to retort.

It's not that I don't want to know,

I don't know where to start.

If only my mere words could show,

the longing of my heart.

Wayward Angel

She wakes up with the light of day,

to set about her task.

It seems sometimes there's just no way,

she can remove her mask.

A little corner office dark,

no sunshine can come through.

She does her best to leave her mark,

as though it were her due.

When day is done and sun has set,

she slips into her car.

She knows she'll soon have no regret,

her reason's not too far.

Arriving home she opens door,

and who should soon appear.

Her daughter whom she does adore,

in joy she sheds a tear.

As nighttime falls and things grow dark,

she gets prepared for bed.

She knows somehow she's left her mark,

her eyelids droop as lead.

Upon her pillow lays her head,

and thanks God for His Grace.

Drifts off to dream with prayers all said,

a glow upon her face.

It's then the mask does fall away,

look closely and you'll see...

A wayward angel here to stay,

no place she'd rather be.

Beast

If only you could see inside,

the beast that I've become.

You would be in for one wild ride,

and likely you'd be numb.

You say you think you know me well,

I'd have to disagree.

Within me the emotions swell,

they beg to be set free.

I seem to be aloof you say,

as if I do not care.

If only I could find a way,

to free them if I dare.

But set them free I darest not,

I fear what they might do.

For in the freedom that it sought,

great pain may come to you.

And so I keep them locked up tight,

that you may not come near.

I pray that they will cause no fright,

to whom I hold so dear.

Lost

I sat there in the warm spring rain,

and pondered what I'd lost.

The memories raged through my brain,

as in a storm were tossed.

That autumn day when we first met,

for dinner and a show.

It was a day I can't forget,

Each detail I do know.

And then there was the night we dined,

above the city lights.

Such beauty we'd be pressed to find,

no matter what the sights.

Or what about the day we fought,

with water guns and kids.

It mattered not how wet we got,

you'd think we'd flipped our lids.

So many memories appear,

from deep within my mind.

Both good and bad they bring a tear,

as joy and pain they find.

I think about the time we passed,

and though it be not long.

Each memory is bound to last,

until I'm dead and gone.

Fool's Price

The cost of love is steep I say,

and oft beyond one's reach.

Of course there is a price to pay,

for all that it does teach.

Not only can you learn pure joy,

but heartache just as well.

Each lesson you will soon employ,

and cause your heart to swell.

Sometimes it swells with love so pure,

as if you are complete.

At times with pain where there's no cure,

your heart just fails to beat.

The cost of love is steep I say,

You'll pay it once or thrice.

And never know until that day,

the sum of the fool's price.

Never Love

I sat and pondered on our love,

and what it meant to me.

It seemed ordained from up above,

as though t'was meant to be.

It seemed as if it mattered not,

the time or locale spent.

Not one moment to be forgot,

as on our journey went.

The close and intimate meeting,

with scarcity of time.

Every precious minute fleeting,

yet each one was sublime.

Or trips together that we took,

at least within our mind.

T'was rivaled not by any book,

on any shelf you'd find.

Two souls blended together be,

so thoroughly as one.

That we've become a melody,

that's only just begun.

Then suddenly I come to see,

reality does shove...

Though perfect we can never be,

My sweetest NeverLove.

True Love

True love is not what you would think,

'tis not an easy thing.

The chains that bind do heavy clink,

and lack a certain bling.

It is not always full of joy,

and sorrows sometimes reign.

But in those times it doth employ,

a smile to hide the pain.

Struggles many must love endure,

its strength put to the test.

But if that love it true and pure,

It's then it shows its best.

For struggles many you will see,

if truly you do love.

But few of them remembered be,

with love from up above.

True love is not what you would think,

for it is full of bliss.

When struggles lost as in a blink,

this point you must not miss.

Glutton

I sat around the table fine,

and did consume my meal.

A perfect night to wine and dine,

there was no better deal.

The appetizers such delight,

and drinks were on the house.

The main course gobbled... every bite,

In Heaven was this louse.

I ate till I could eat no more,

and drank till I was drunk.

Then suddenly my belly sore,

I felt like such a punk.

The meal and drink were free you see,

and yet they had their cost.

A rift it caused for you and me,

I pray not all is lost.

For the meal is my anger see,

the drink.. the words that flow.

So no more will I dine with glee,

but pray with head held low.

Prison

I'm locked here in these prison walls,

there's no way out it seems.

My tears they flow as anguished squalls,

and wash away my dreams.

It's oh so very lonely here,

this cell where I'm confined.

I long for ones I hold so dear,

and pray they do not mind.

So here in solitude I sit,

and ponder on my way.

I hope someday that I am fit,

to see the light of day.

But till the day that I am free,

and then my sentence done.

I'll keep my pain inside of me,

this prison made for one.

War

I sit here in the silent night,

my mind a tad bit numb.

And ponder be it wrong or right,

on what I shall become.

I think of the success I've had,

and all the failures too.

The many times my heart was glad,

and those that were so blue.

Though many battles have I seen,

and many have I lost.

From each of them did knowledge glean,

each scar was worth the cost.

For it is not the battles see,

of which I'm keeping score.

The secret between you and me...

I'm out to win the war.

So as I ponder on this night,

just what I might become.

I swear I'll never cease to fight,

until my war is done.

Torn

I knowest not what I should do,

the choices hurt my brain.

It seems as if I have no clue,

I may just go insane.

There is the one my heart desires,

love's arrow has struck deep.

Impossible to quench the fires,

not even as I sleep.

But then my brain doth agitate,

against my heart conspire.

With logic must annihilate,

and snuff the raging fire.

And so in a conundrum be,

my very being is torn.

I pray someday I shall be free,

and true love may be born.

But till that time I have no clue,

I'll take it day by day.

And hope somehow someway that you,

will help me find the way.

Masen

My oh my what could this be,

this thing I hold so close to me?

A precious gift did God impart,

as silent praises fill my heart.

I gaze upon his angelic face,

surrounded it is by Heaven's grace.

My cheek against his skin so soft,

sends my spirit soaring aloft.

Slowly now he opens his eyes,

looks at me... utters no cries.

I ask myself why I've been stressing,

When God has given me such a blessing.

I wrap him up tight and neat,

and listen to his little heart beat.

Giving thanks to Father and Son,

for a precious baby grandson.

Mother

What dear Mother can I say,

when I contemplate the price you pay.

You always wanted the best for me,

though stubborn I was, oft did not see.

You gently taught me right from wrong,

and a lesson learned seldom took long.

Though perfect I could never be,

Unconditional was your love for me.

Even now in my middle years,

No matter the problem you lend me your ears.

And even though my own life I run,

A Mother's job is never done.

So what dear Mother can I do,

To show my admiring love for you?

Perhaps a poet's heart can say,

I love you Mom, Happy Mother's Day.

In Memoriam

I sat alone one summer's eve,

basking in the sun.

Pondering how remembered be,

when my time on earth was done.

Thoughts of careless mistakes once made,

of the loved ones I had pained.

For some with grace had let them fade,

yet so many more remained.

Then on to the victories my mind did rush,

so many accolades won.

The mistakes grew faint as victories did crush,

and I felt the warmth of the sun.

But just as I thought I had figured it out,

an abrupt moment of clarity.

My thoughts about me had no true clout,

and indeed should be such a rarity.

For it was then I realized with rather a fright,

that neither of them matter not.

What matters is your inner light,

and the causes for which you fought.

I'd pray you heed these words so tender,

if I had my druthers.

For the only thing those left remember,

Is the good we did for others.

Demon's Disguise

Be careful young man as you progress,

for you have much to discern...

Demons menace the darkness...

conspiring to consume your soul.

Silently they lie in contemplation...

plotting their evil schemes,

as though you were the ultimate prize.

Casting their lots, betting the odds

that you will fall into their clutches...

Your heart pounds in terror

as you seek rescue from the darkness...

But lo, a bright light appears...

the darkness dissipates rapidly,

and demons scatter in terror...

fleeing you for their very lives.

Light slowly comes into focus,

and before you she stands...

radiant in all of her glory.

Her loveliness beyond exquisite...

she approaches you slowly,

mesmerizing you with her gaze.

She wraps her tender arms around you...

bringing you close to her bosom,

caressing you with the softest of touch.

Collapsing slowly into her arms,

you finally feel safe from the terrors

which have plagued you for so long.

But be careful young man,

you have much to learn...

For the most evil of demons,

is one we oft not distinguish...

She is easy on the eyes,

and appears as an angel...

Yet she will play hell with your heart…

Cancer

Cancer...

You filthy tempestuous infirmity!

You have the audacity to afflict...

to attempt our demise?

A scourge upon the earth are you!

Power you exert in baneful ways,

draining wellness and spirit.

A challenge you issue menacingly...

taunting, prodding us to relent

and succumb to your desires...

mocking us in our defiance,

hopelessness is your mantra.

Yet the battle rages on...

fueled by the will to triumph

over our common foe.

Many a number have we lost...

stolen from us before their time

by your evil minions.

Friends, loved ones, children...

Your evil knows no boundaries,

No mercy do you possess.

But inefficacious your effort shall be,

as long as one of us remains...

It is your demise that is one day certain,

your evil banished eternally.

But until that glorious victory be,

There is but one thing I can say for me...

I WILL KICK YOUR ASS!

Memorial Day

In remembrance we set aside this day,

and have kept it many years.

To honor those who paved the way,

with blood and sweat and tears.

Fathers..sons..and many a brother,

have given it their all.

Tears wiped away from wife or mother,

of loved ones who took the fall.

Mothers..daughters..and sisters too,

gave all they had to give.

In the glorious name of red, white, and blue,

so under freedom we may live.

It has no bearing which battle or war,

these heroes they did serve.

Belief in our country was part of their core,

from their duty did not swerve.

And so this day we give thanks and praise,

to heroes present and past.

Because of them the Flag we raise,

may freedom forever last.

Family

We are a family don't you see,

to one another bound.

Oh, surely though it cannot be,

since no lineage can be found.

No common father or mother,

to me it makes no mind.

Not even "really" sister or brother,

I think of you in kind.

There is no strand of my DNA,

not one characteristic to be found.

I do not know what to say,

as to why we're so closely bound.

Some I have raised as my own,

without a second thought.

With pride I have seen them grown,

now living as they ought.

Others may a lover have been,

at a give point in time.

And I would do it over again,

for the lessons I learned sublime.

Still others only a friend may be,

time together long or short.

For time matters not you see,

When you have a good report.

Then there are those I have yet to meet,

for now we only "chat".

I pray someday I get to greet,

from someplace other than I sat.

It matters not the role you play,

how very big or small.

It is simply that you made me stay,

and in life give my all.

I pray you get my point you see,

more than blood or flesh.

I consider you my family,

as in life we did enmesh.

Seasons

The seasons begin anew,

winter awakens from silence...

no longer basking in warmth,

but cast out into the cold...

long and painful at times,

yet immense beauty it brings.

Winter fades to spring,

the cycle of growth begins...

higher and stronger,

longing to be so much more...

but its seed not yet ripe,

and in tenderness must remain.

With summer comes strength,

full growth and power reached...

much is accomplished now,

the time of most production...

bursting forth to multiply,

ensuring its own continuation.

At long last comes fall,

growth slows and wanes...

the color slowly fades,

moving forward to the end...

life force finally drains,

and winter arrives again.

So is the cycle of seasons...

so are the cycles of life...

Father

I sat today to contemplate,

about a father I once did hate.

Adopted me when I was young,

but praise from him was never sung.

His method of control was fear,

the feeling of love never near.

And so I grew up by and by,

hidden in myself and very shy.

Then one day it came to be,

when finally I was set free.

I started doing what I could,

oft ignoring what I should.

And so began a quick decline,

thinking the only way was mine.

Myself and others through the years,

causing and shedding many tears.

Until alone one drunken night,

I cried to God to hear my plight.

In fierce anger at Him did yell,

begging for answers that He might tell.

Then in the darkness to me He came,

and within my heart stuck His claim.

Within me you could find no fear,

unending peace as He drew me near.

Since then many years have passed,

my hatred simply couldn't last.

For in my years I came to see,

my father taught me what not to be.

Now since that time I've raised my own,

and I'm very proud of how they've grown.

All praise goes to my one true Father,

without Whom I would never bother.

Happy Father's Day...

Fighter

Sometimes life's a long hard road,

with many a twist and turn.

And oft times such a heavy load,

and painful lessons to learn.

Life throws a ball and it's a curve,

you wonder what the hell.

Whatever purpose could this serve,

and upon it you may dwell.

You won't give up you push on through,

as tough as it may get.

It's harder than you ever knew,

and against you they may bet.

But still you rise above the fray,

you have to emerge on top.

To you it's just another day,

proof you're cream of the crop.

Never give up... never say die,

your fists clench only tighter.

And if they dare to ask you why,

the answer, "I'm a Fighter."

Just In Case

Just in case tomorrow,

never again we speak...

Don't hang your head in sorrow,

not a single tear let leak.

We always knew this day would come,

just didn't know the time...

So if indeed my life is done,

I've lived a life sublime.

You know you meant the world to me,

family, lover, or friend...

And never will that change you see,

not even in the end.

It matters not the time we knew,

how much we had together...

Just know I'll always be with you,

in spirit and forever.

So put a smile upon your face,

and remember me in your heart.

Surrounded by our Good Lord's grace,

as in Heaven I make my start.

About the Author

Jon Burgess

Jon Burgess began his journey into the world of poetry in late 2011, and it was an idea he would have scoffed at not long before, having had a total belief that his family's artistic gene had completely passed him by. What began merely as an attempt to put some feelings to paper during a trying time proved to be a therapeutic catharsis which soon encompassed not only his life but lives of friends, loved ones, and the events of today's world.

In addition to his newest endeavor, he is also a Registered Nurse, specializing in Home Care for the elderly and a self-employed entrepreneur who enjoys traveling for both business and pleasure.

He is also a proud father and grandfather. In his spare time, he enjoys reading, travel, playing games, spending time with loved ones, and virtually anything out in the sun. He is also a notoriously diehard Seahawks fan.

CUSTER'S LOST SCOUT

JOHN KOSTER

Idle Winter Press
Portland, Oregon

Idle Winter Press
Portland, Oregon
http://IdleWinter.com

This edition published 2017
Printed in the United States of America
The text of this book is in Alegreya

ISBN-13: 978-1945687020 (Idle Winter Press)
ISBN-10: 1945687029

CONTENTS

INTRODUCTION

This is the story of Left Hand, a Hunkpapa Sioux, who served General George Armstrong Custer as a guide, scout, and messenger during the campaign that ended at Custer's Last Stand.

Left Hand was given an honored funeral by the warriors who fought Custer. Government records and primary sources document Left Hand's service as a scout and warrior, but the reasons behind this service remain a mystery. Left Hand was a member of the subtribe of the Sioux Nation known as the Hunkpapa Lakota, part of the Standing Rock Sioux Tribe.

Through conversations with my friend John Eagle Shield (a relative of Sitting Bull and Medical Director of the Standing Rock Sioux Tribe), my own knowledge of the Battle of the Little Bighorn, and a rudimentary understanding of Lakota language and customs, I was able to piece together what happened.

Some questions remain, but the fact that Left Hand joined the U.S. Army, honorably served out his full enlistment, rejoined his own people just before the Battle of the Little Bighorn, and died defending the Sioux and Cheyenne from Custer is recorded by the Hunkpapa Lakota at Standing Rock.

— John Koster

THE ENLISTMENT

The baby was crying again. The cries hurt Left Hand's heart and burned in his belly. No man likes the sound of a baby crying.

Women were supposed to keep them quiet. But Left Hand knew that the baby was crying because she was hungry. He knew it was his failure as a hunter and as a husband that kept the baby hungry. His wife said nothing, but she knew it too. Left Hand burned with shame beneath his buffalo robe, the last one he hadn't traded for flour and lard. He wished he could leave the cabin but it was too cold to sleep outside.

Once again, Left Hand turned it over in his thoughts.

Bloody Knife, who was a Húŋkpapȟa Lakȟóta—on his father's side anyway, though his mother was a Pȟaláni [Arikara] like Left Hand's wife—had told Left Hand that Long Hair and his brother Little Hair wanted to find other scouts who could speak Lakȟóta and who knew the Black Hills and the Big Horn country. Left Hand had been considering it. Long Hair was a great warrior chief, but the people hated Little Hair, and Left Hand was leery of Bloody Knife.

The Húŋkpapȟa people at home had said that Bloody Knife's Pȟaláni mother was the daughter of a marriage between first cousins. The thought made Left Hand's flesh crawl. His own wife's grandparents had not been relatives. One grandfather was Lakȟóta. Left Hand had made sure of that. Cousin marriage led to weak and sickly children, or strange crazy children, and he believed the Lakȟóta were a greater people than the Pȟaláni, though his wife was a good woman.

Left Hand thought Bloody Knife actually looked like a white man with an Indian's skin.(1) Gall, the Húŋkpapȟa war chief, had given Bloody Knife a brutal beating the last time Bloody Knife had visited the Húŋkpapȟa Village and had driven him out.

Grandchildren of married cousins were not welcome. Bloody Knife had gone to live with the Pȟaláni, his mother's people. Then he went to live with the whites. Now he was Long Hair's favorite scout.

Left Hand made up his mind. He would talk to Bloody Knife.

A warrior's first duty was to feed his family. If a man fed his wives and their children, then his wives would work hard and remain faithful. If he failed them, his wives took their children back to their grandfather and grandmother, or looked for other men. The shame of failure would be worse than being a friend of Bloody Knife. *No man*, Left Hand thought, *should be blamed for who his father or mother had been, or for their mistakes.*

With this decision, he curled up and slept better. As the sun came up, the worst of the bitter cold lifted. Left Hand threw off his robe and straightened his clothing.

"Today I will find a way to get food," he said.

His wife peered at him. "How?"

"I will touch the pen and join the soldiers."

She nodded slowly. "This is not easy for you, but the baby must eat."

"You, too, must eat," Left Hand said. "I must eat, too. If I eat with the soldiers, I will bring you back a biscuit."

They both smiled. His wife loved biscuits, but to make them, you had to put the soft dough in an iron pan. Biscuits were a treat. She usually fried the dough in melted fat in a round iron pot and the dough tasted wet.

Left Hand whipped out his belt knife and sliced a long piece from the flitch of hard, dried Indian Agency beef. He left his wife the better half of the dried meat, hung up out of the reach of stray dogs. Issue Day was coming soon and she could get flour then, and more beef, and coffee that sometimes had dirt mixed in it by the white men who put it in the sack. His wife sometimes used a marrow-cracker to break up the lumps in the flour. But if you cooked it with grease it filled your stomach, and the baby could eat it in small bites. They both looked at the baby, asleep in her cradle board.

"Meat is too tough for the little one. I can boil some bones for soup," his wife said.

"Now she sleeps," Left Hand said with a smile, "but I know what I must do." Left Hand picked up his musket and his shot pouch. The whites must know that he owned a gun and not just a bow and arrows. "If they give out tobacco, trade it for more flour or beef," he said as an afterthought.

She nodded and they gazed at one another. Left Hand slung his horse rope around his neck rope and wrapped his robe around himself, shaking it down. He stepped out of the cottonwood cabin and walked along the river until he caught his horse.(2)

Left Hand rode all through the daylight. The plains were cold and bleak, and there was not much to see. He wished for a stray antelope—or even a coyote, though coyote was tough, sinewy meat, tougher than an old dog. You felt sad when you ate a dog, if you knew him when he was alive. But he saw nothing to eat.

On the afternoon of the third day Left Hand saw the white man's fort of big houses with little houses on top. The houses looked like short, fat men with crooked hats on top for soldiers to hide in during snow and wind, or fight from behind logs in case of trouble. But Left Hand knew that the wagon guns that stood like watchdogs waiting to bite were more to be feared than soldiers who hid in houses. The wagon guns shot bullets as big as a man's head or rotten bullets that blew up like a bad gun blows up in the hand.

Nobody looked twice as Left Hand rode in. The blue-coat soldiers walked around in twos and threes, and white women in their funny dresses that looked like drooping flowers walked in pairs or with their children. Left Hand rode to the long log house where the scouts lived. He saw Bloody Knife with some other Indian scouts. Bloody Knife had a straight nose, neither long nor short, and a curl to his lip—he always looked as if he wanted to insult someone. Sometimes he insulted white people and told them how foolish they were.(3) Long Hair thought this was funny. Bloody Knife looked up. He knew Left Hand by sight. He wore only one keepsake: a small steel horseshoe he kept in his cartridge belt.

"Háu, kȟolá," Left Hand said. He called Bloody Knife *friend* as smoothly as he could. It was too much to use the word *brother* for a man whose grandparents were cousins.

Bloody Knife seemed to sense this but he smiled —that strange sarcastic smile with a hard glint in his eye that said, *I know you don't like me and you know I don't like you.*

"Háu, Napé Čhatká," Bloody Knife said. When an experienced warrior remembered your name it was an honor. He had no grudge with Bloody Knife now, and his wife and baby needed to eat.

"What do you come here for, hokšíla?" Bloody Knife asked. Being called a young man by an older man was not an honor, but not an insult either. Left Hand felt that Bloody Knife was testing him.

"Huŋká, my wife and daughter are hungry," Left Hand said. "I want to be a scout for Long Hair and Bloody Knife."

"Oháŋ! Líla wašté!" Bloody Knife said. "Come to the soldier house and we will touch the pen."

"Philámayaye, huŋká," Left Hand said. His relief and gratitude were genuine. There was no harm in thanking an uncle who helped your family.

Bloody Knife smiled his curling, snide smile and his eyes glinted. "After we touch the pen, we will eat..." Bloody Knife said.

"Philámayaye, huŋká . . ." Left Hand said, trying not to sound too pathetic.

"After we eat, we will find you a real gun," Bloody Knife said with quiet laughter in his stomach. His lip never seemed to uncurl itself.

The soldiers' house was long and dark. A fat white man with a blue coat and brown hair growing out of his face sat at a table. Bloody Knife and the man conversed in a mixture gestures and a language Left Hand could not understand. The words sounded more like English than Pȟaláni.

Left Hand studied the white man. Nobody was skinny in this place, and he could tell from the man's breath that the soldiers had money for whiskey as well as food.

"Nitúwe huwó?" Bloody Knife asked abruptly, with a glimmer of mischief. The soldier was asking Left Hand who he was.

"Napé Čhatká emáčiyapi weló," Left Hand said. *I am Left Hand.*

"Lakȟóta heníčha he?" the fat white man asked. *Are you a Sioux?* Left Hand was surprised but he concealed it. The white man was smarter than he looked.

"Háŋ, Lakȟóta akíčhita hemáčha weló," Left Hand said proudly. Yes, I am an experienced Sioux warrior. Suddenly he wondered if the soldier would want to know if Left Hand had killed any others who might have been relatives. He decided to talk less and let Blood Knife insult these white people to his heart's content.

The blue-coat with the hair on his face set a piece of white paper in front of Bloody Knife. He pushed a little black pot with a stick in it toward Left Hand.

"Make the mark," Bloody Knife said.

Left Hand had seen inkwells before but had never used one. He lifted the little stick to find a metal blade covered with very black water. He understood the use of it: when you pressed the stick to the paper, the black water made a mark.

The fat white man pointed to a line next to a strange picture that looked like a flower. Left Hand bent forward and drew a picture of a left hand with the thumb inside. The fat white man smiled. *He is not stupid at all*, Left Hand thought. *He is a human with white skin, but the brownish hair sprouting out of the back of his white hand is disgusting.*

The fat white man stood halfway up, bent slightly forward and stuck out his hand. Left Hand knew the gesture and stuck out his own hand—but he was left-handed and the white man had to change hands to shake. Left Hand could have pulled him off balance as a joke but that would be rude. Bloody Knife's face betrayed his amusement at their consternation.

"Uŋyíŋ kte," Bloody Knife said. *Let's get moving.* Bloody Knife and Left Hand walked back out into the cold.

"You forgot the most important thing in dealing with white men," Bloody Knife said.

"What is that?" Left Hand asked.

"You forgot to ask how much money you get," Bloody Knife said.

"It seemed rude," Left Hand said. Actually, he hadn't thought of it.

"They will give you sixteen dollars a month and twelve more for your horse," Bloody Knife said. (4)

"Is that good or bad?" Left Hand asked. He had lived among the Húŋkpapȟa with Sitting Bull and seen few whites before meeting his young Pȟaláni wife at Fort Berthold, where he had stayed to court and marry her.

"A white soldier gets thirteen dollars a month, but they give him the horse," Bloody Knife said.

"Héčhetu weló," Left Hand said. *That is right.* "We are better warriors than the whites . . . but they have bigger horses." He added quickly. "But you are a bigger warrior than I am."

"Come to dinner," Bloody Knife said.

The white soldiers were all standing in a line in a long low building with long tables and many chairs. Some fat white men with large, strange breechclouts stood at one end doling out food. The breechclouts reached almost to their chins instead of hanging down to their knees like a Lakȟóta breechclout. Bloody Knife and Left Hand stood in line next to the last of the soldiers. Guests were not fed first here, but it was not an insult—just the way white people did things.

Left Hand could tell that the soldiers didn't like Indians much but that they were also afraid of them. Bloody Knife was not a tall man but he was strongly built. Left Hand was taller. He had wrestled other Lakȟóta boys from the time he was five or six years old, on foot or on horseback. The boys shot mud-balls at the girls, and then fled when the girls chased the younger boys and hit them with hockey sticks. The boys burned themselves by sticking pine seeds to their wrists and setting them on fire so they could face pain without crying or changing expressions. Left Hand had started hunting buffalo on horseback in his early teens. (4) He knew he was a better warrior than the white men—on horseback or on foot. They were right to be afraid of him, but he tried not to be rude. This was their camp and he was a guest who had come without gifts, even if he had to wait for his food.

As he looked at his tin plate, one white man ladled on a dollop of beans, one gave him a large biscuit, and one gave him a hefty piece of roasted meat. The last man filled Left Hand's tin cup with black coffee.

Left Hand looked askance at the chairs—he had never sat on one—and Bloody Knife nodded him outside. Another Lakȟóta he knew by sight, an older man named Running Bear In The Timber, was sitting on the step outside. They all nodded and grunted greetings.

"Bad at home?" Running Bear asked, sympathetically.

Left Hand nodded. "The Issue never lasts through the month and the food is not good."

"Once it was worse," Running Bear said. "When the old agent came to us, he brought everything he owned in a little bag. When he left, it took two steamboats to carry it all away." (5)

"A man must feed his wife and child," Left Hand said. He slipped the biscuit into his shot pouch and ate the meat and beans.

(1)   Connell, Evan S., SON OF THE MORNING STAR, Page 17, for Bloody Knife's appearance and history. The Lakota dread of incest, general among American Indians, is common knowledge.

(2)   Tracy Potter of the Fort Abraham Lincoln Foundation says, confirming Elizabeth Custer in "Boots and Saddles," that the Arikara and intermarried Lakota who sometimes served as scouts lived in a tipi village near Fort Berthold, about 100 miles from Fort Abraham Lincoln.

(3)   Connell, Evan S., SON OF THE MORNING STAR, Page 17, description by William Eleroy Curtis of the *Chicago Inter Ocean*.

(4)   Neihardt, John G., BLACK ELK SPEAKS: BEING THE LIFE STORY OF A HOLY MAN OF THE OGLALA SIOUX, Page 15

(5)   Smith, Jean Edward, GRANT, Page 526. Actual quote from Charles Lewis Slattery, FELIX REVILLE BRUNOT.

WHY THEY WERE HUNGRY

When Francis Parkman lived with the Sioux on a vacation from Harvard, he had only one serious complaint about their hospitality—they over-fed him. Parkman enjoyed talking with the older men and the warriors of his own age, but the conversations had their distractions.

"We were also infested by little copper-colored naked boys and snake-eyed girls," Parkman wrote of his life among the Sioux in 1846. "They would come up to us and muttering certain words, which being interpreted conveyed the concise invitation, 'Come and eat.'

Then we would rise, cursing the pertinacity of Dakota hospitality, which allowed scarcely an hour of rest between sun and sun, and to which we were bound to do honor unless we would offend our entertainers. This necessity was particularly burdensome to me, as I was scarcely able to walk from the effects of illness, and was poorly qualified to dispose of twenty meals a day." (1)

While Parkman was in camp, an Indian brought in a starving runaway slave from Texas he had found on the plains. The French trappers with Parkman made the man a bowl of gruel, and after the first taste the slave began to ask for meat. The trappers warned him to eat slowly—gorging after prolonged starvation can split the stomach and cause death. The trappers' Indian wives brought him small pieces of meat and turnips to gradually restore his strength. "When it grew dark he contrived to creep away between the legs of the horses and crawl over to the Indian camp. There he fed to his heart's content . . . he expressed his firm conviction that nothing could ever kill him." (2)

Even as Easterners were reading "The Oregon Trail," and Henry Wadsworth Longfellow's "Hiawatha," the days when the Sioux had more food than they needed for themselves and their guests was rumbling gradually to a close. Parkman himself had seen wagon trails headed for Oregon or the Mormon settlements in

Utah. The white emigrants and the Sioux—Lakȟóta in their own language, roughly: "alliance of friends"— generally got along peacefully.

The settlers themselves barely made a dent in the vast buffalo herds when they dared to hunt instead of simply trading for wild game with friendly Indians. But the presence of trading posts that provided goods the Indians needed—muskets, axes, steel knives, cooking pots—and the increasing flow of settlers brought on by the opening of California began a cycle in which settlers and Indians alike killed too many buffalo for the buffalo to maintain the size of their vast herds.

After a clash between headstrong young men on both sides, the Sioux and the United States fought their first war in 1854 – 1855. In the aftermath, the astounded Oglala Sioux received their first Indian Agent: Thomas Twiss, second in his class at West Point in 1826, later an instructor at the United States Military Academy, and then a college professor of mathematics and philosophy for 18 years at the University of South Carolina. Twiss had ventured into manufacturing and failed. His wife, an early advocate of advanced education for women, had suffered a nervous breakdown. Professor Twiss was forced to leave her in the care of their youngest daughter and head West to seek his fortune. (3)

Twiss had been unimpressed by the Lakota at first, but an incident turned him around. After an attack on a mail coach, the Lakota were ordered to hand over the attackers or face another conflict with the soldiers. General William Harney had already attacked a Lakota camp at Ash Hollow in the middle of negotiations and killed about 86 men, women, and children, mostly with howitzers. Since the Lakota had no match for artillery with exploding shells, they decided on peace.

The Indians handed over five volunteers to expiate the attack on the mail coach: Red Chief and Long Chin, brothers of Chief Conquering Bear, shot in the back during a misunderstanding in 1854, their cousin Spotted Tail, and two other warriors who had volunteered to take the place of two teenagers who had joined in the attack on the mail coach. The grown men were willing to die so that the boys could live to maturity. The five hostages dressed and painted themselves for death, fully expecting to be hanged or shot.

Twiss, mightily impressed, sent the five Lakota to Fort Leavenworth, Kansas in chains, but he also wrote a letter to the Indian Office telling both sides of the story. President Franklin Pierce pardoned all five Indians and sent then back to their people alive and with gifts. Thomas Twiss became a white man the Lakota trusted.

General Harney, brutal as he was in combat, also heard both sides, and began to support Twiss in an effort to foster peace between the Lakota and the whites. "With proper management a new era will dawn upon such of the Indians as yet remain," Harney wrote. "The Sioux seek it and look forward to it with a hope which I trust may not be blighted. They have been deceived so often by the whites that they would never again give them their confidence." He ordered the Lakota and their allies not to venture north of the Platte River to interfere with the wagon train routes or small settlements.

The Lakota and their allies, the Northern Cheyenne and the Northern Arapaho, kept the peace except for a few outcasts or troublesome youngsters. But increased hunting by white settlers was reducing the buffalo and antelope herds to such an extent that the Indians came to understand that their way of life was in jeopardy and that their actual lives were also at risk. The Indians spoke to Twiss about the vanishing game and the poor hunting, and on September 18, 1859, at his agency at Deer Creek, Thomas Twiss proposed a vast change in Indian policy to the Indians themselves:

fixed reservations and farming instead of simply accepting gifts to keep the peace.

"My Children, your Great Father directs me to say to you that as the buffalo and small game also are rapidly diminishing, what do you propose to do to gain subsistence, where there is no longer any game for food, and prevent your old people and little children from dying of starvation? Will you labor like the white man, plant, hoe, and raise corn for food? Or will you die of hunger?" (4)

The chiefs of the three tribes appointed a wise old Arapaho, named Medicine Man, as their spokesman and conferred with him about their wishes.

"Our country for hunting game has become very small," Medicine Man said. "Our old people and little children are hungry for many days, and some die; for our hunters caught no meat. Our sufferings are increasing every winter. Our horses, too, are dying because we ride them so far to get a little game for our Lodges. We want to live."

Twiss and the Indians worked out the details of which land would be set aside and protected for each tribe. The Northern Arapaho agreed to accept land on the Cache la Poudre River, the Northern Cheyenne on the Laramie, the Oglala Lakota on Horse Creek and

Deer Creek and the Brule and other western Lakota on the White River east of the Black Hills.

"Father, we give all the rest of our country to our Great Father," Medicine Man said. "It is no longer any use to us as most of the game has disappeared." (6)

Twiss and the Indians then drew up a proposed formal treaty which would provide the three tribes who signed with $115,000 a year from Washington in goods, farming equipment, and contracted assistance "for a period at the discretion of the President of the United States." The Indians all signed in one day. Congress rejected the treaty because it was too expensive.

When the Civil War broke out, troops had to be recalled from the forts, and frontier militia units manned some of the garrisons. Fighting soon broke out all over the West. Indians and white frontier militiamen both sought revenge for past wrongs. At the end of the Civil War in the East, the government patched up a series of treaties with the Plains Indians but then offended the Sioux and Cheyenne by building three forts in territory that had been promised to the Indians a few months before.

Twiss was by now informally married to a Lakota girl named Mary Standing Elk, and reportedly told her father, Chief Standing Elk, not to accept the white men's road and the forts built to protect them.

Standing Elk told Red Cloud. What followed was Red Cloud's War, the Indian war that the Lakota, Cheyenne, and Arapaho actually won. For parts of three years, the Indians fought the soldiers to a standstill.

At the end the United States decided, as it was said, that "it was cheaper to feed them than to fight them." The Sioux Treaty of 1868 established land officially set aside for the Indians and regular payments so that the tribes could become farmers and craftsmen and send their children to school to "look in books."

Ulysses S. Grant became president in 1868, and the man defamed as "a butcher" for fighting the Civil War to a bloody but final conclusion showed himself to be surprisingly humane when it came to Indian policy. Grant had no patience with the suggestion of the Darwinians that the Indians were doomed to extinction as hopeless primitives.

"I do not believe our Creator ever placed the different races on this earth with a view of having the strong exert all his energies in exterminating the weak," (7) Grant told George H. Stuart, one of the influential millionaires and humanitarians he appointed to the Board of Indian Commissioners. This Board was a group which set out to reform the growing corruption of what came to be known as "The Indian Ring"—

swindlers who stole the supplies they were supposed to be handing out to the tribes.

The Episcopal Bishop of Minnesota, Henry B. Whipple, noted that it was "a tradition of the frontier that an Indian agent with $1,500 a year could retire upon an ample fortune in three years." Or, as the Indian told General William Tecumseh Sherman about this time, agents who arrived with a carpetbag needed two steamboats to haul away their belongings after just a few years. Grant appointed Quakers and other religious men as Indian agents. But the old agents used political influence to stay in place because the pickings were so good—and they won support by passing some of their loot up the ladder.

Ely S. Parker, a remarkably self-educated Seneca Indian, self-taught as both a lawyer and a licensed engineer, and a personal friend of Grant's, was ironically brought up on charges of corruption even though he was exonerated by a full Congressional investigation. (8) Parker's real crime to some people in government was that he had married a respectable white woman half his own age, an unforgivable offense even though he was a Civil War veteran who had actually written out the draft to Robert E. Lee's surrender for Grant at Appomattox when Grant had a migraine headache. Lee had shaken hands with him and called him a real American.

The next two Indian Commissioners, Edward P. Smith and John Q. Smith, both left the office under suspicion of wrongdoing, though they never faced charges as the educated Indian Ely S. Parker had. (9)

Long criticized by the Indians themselves and by frontier clergymen and some Army officers, the Indian Bureau finally got some national exposure through an unlikely agent: Dinosaur Hunter Othniel Marsh. The pioneer paleontologist needed a safe conduct and an escort to hunt for fossils in unceded Sioux country and had contacted Red Cloud, the Oglala chief who had defeated the Army in Red Cloud's War and obtained a guaranteed reservation and regular food as conditions of the Sioux Treaty of 1868. Marsh was given Lakota permission to hunt fossils in the White River Badlands. In return, Chief Red Cloud asked Professor Marsh to take some other specimens back to Washington—examples of what the Oglala and Brule received from their agent, J.J. Saville. Red Cloud gave Marsh samples of bad flour, maggoty pork, and spoiled sugar, coffee and tobacco. (10)

Marsh displayed the specimens in Washington and showed them to Indian Commission Edward P. Smith, who showed scant interest. Marsh then took his story right up to President Grant. The New York Herald, the leading Democratic newspaper of the day, heard about the story and used to it lambast Grant, a Republican, along with Secretary of the Interior Columbus Delano and Indian Commissioner Edward P. Smith, who resigned.

General George Armstrong Custer—a Civil War hero and a Democrat—praised Marsh as a disinterested witness. Custer said that most people on the frontier knew that Indian agents were corrupt and offered some examples. Marsh published a 36-page pamphlet in which he asserted that some of the 13,000 Sioux at the agencies had literally starved and frozen due to graft in the Indian Service. Marsh also addressed an open letter to President Grant: "You alone have the will and the power to destroy the combination of bad men, known as the Indian ring, who are debasing this service and thwarting the efforts of all who endeavor to bring to full consummation your noble policy of peace."

Delano and Saville also resigned— no one was able to prove that Columbus Delano himself had stolen a dime, but his son got some lucrative contracts from surveyors measuring the boundaries of Indian Reservations which seemed to make the reservations smaller and smaller by the year—even though the son never showed up for work. (12) But most of the crooked agents hung on for dear life, unwilling to give up lucrative positions where the U.S. Army could be called out to protect their right to steal in case the Indians lost their tempers.

The newspapers printed stories. The kindly clergymen protested. But on Issue Day, so much of the food had vanished between Washington and the agencies that the Indians seldom got enough food to make it through the month.

(1)   Parkman, Francis, THE OREGON TRAIL, Page 120

(2)   Ibid, Pages 124-126

(3)   Nadeau, Remi. FORT LARAMIE AND THE INDIANS,
115-116, 125-128

(4)   Ibid, Page 144

(5)   Ibid, Page 144

(6)   Ibid, Page 145

(7)   Smith, Jean Edward, GRANT, Page 524

(8)   Ibid, Page 540

(9)   Ibid, Page 540

(10)   Wallace, David Raines, THE BONEHUNTERS;
REVENGE, Page 100

(11)   Ibid, 104

(12)   AMERICAN NATIONAL BIOGRAPHY, article on
Columbus Delano, Volume 6, Page 379

AT THE SOLDIERS' HOUSE

Left Hand's wife was thrilled when she saw the soldiers' house set up for the Pȟaláni [Arikara] scouts and their families at Fort Lincoln. The scouts and their wives and children lived in a long, low, log barracks with bunks and sections cordoned off for each family. The Indians were given bunk beds, but those who were suspicious of furniture because it kept them from the earth slept instead on the earthen floor. A big stone fireplace at one end blazed with logs—the soldiers' house was never cold—and it always smelled of good food and Indian tobacco. (1) Left Hand was proud of being able to feed his wife and baby again, to keep them warm, and to make sure they had plenty of friends.

The soldiers must have known that the Indians had plenty of food so they never came looking to buy the Indian girls. The girls, in turn, knew that the soldiers had diseases that led to sick or dead babies and made women old and ugly before their time, so they kept away from the soldiers.

A few days after Left Hand brought his wife to Fort Lincoln, Bloody Knife told Left Hand to follow him to the white medicine man's house. A few Pȟaláni [Arikara] were lined up and an older white man with no hair on top, glass things in front of his eyes, and a white coat gestured at them.

"Left Hand," Bloody Knife said in English. Left Hand recognized the name. Bloody Knife told Left Hand to strip to the breechclout. Left Hand flung his robe over a chair, slipped off his moccasins, untied his leggings, and took off his shirt. The doctor looked him over, smiled, and poked him in a few places, with a friendly smile to show this was not an insult. (2) The doctor nodded and said something to another fat old soldier, who made marks in a book.

"He says you are a good man, good for a soldier," Bloody Knife said.

"Philámayaye, huŋká," Left Hand said to the white doctor. *Thank you, Uncle.* Respect for his elders was respect for himself, and he liked the old white man with no hair on top.

"Was he scalped?" Left Hand asked Bloody Knife softly in Lakȟóta.

Bloody Knife smiled his snide, curling smile and answered "no" with his eyes.

"Their hair falls out by itself," he said. "So do their teeth."

"The women too?" Left Hand asked with a slight chill and a mild creeping disgust in his belly.

"The women don't lose their hair, unless they get diseases," Bloody Knife said.

"I think a Lakȟóta woman would rather die than live without hair," Left Hand said uneasily.

"Some of them buy other women's hair and make it into hats." Bloody Knife said. Left Hand saw the sense of that.

As soon as Left Hand had put his clothes back on, Bloody Knife led him to a long table with some of the Pȟaláni. Soldiers handed him a blue hat with a feather, a dark blue woolen soldier coat with brass buttons, light blue woolen soldier leggings with no space for a breechclout, two cotton shirts, two cotton leggings with no breechclout, a grey flannel shirt, and heavy rough shoes. Last of all, they handed him a heavy sky-blue woolen coat with a cape. Left Hand had never owned so much new clothing in his life.

Next, a soldier offered a gun with a long barrel and three brass bands, like the white foot-soldiers carried. Left Hand knew this was a strong gun and loaded from the back but he was not sure how to do this. The soldier gave Left hand a heavy cloth bag and a heavy cloth belt with loops for bullets. Left Hand was amazed at the clothing and the rifle, which together were worth one or two horses. The soldiers also gave him a tin cup and a tin plate. (3) He had no words to express his gratitude at the generosity of the white men, and how proud he was to be a soldier for them.

Left Hand's wife and the other women in the soldiers' house were happy to discover that the scouts and their families were given all kinds of food—the scout leaders brought fresh bread, thick hardtack crackers in little squares, coffee, bacon, beans, sugar, and tea. The women were curious about the dry strips of hard vegetables that had to be cut like dried meat and boiled in pots. When the strips were cooked, they broke down into cabbage and bean soup. Though this food was new and wonderful to Left Hand's wife, not all of it was tasty. The fresh beef and the fresh bread were always good. (4)

One night, Bloody Knife told the scouts that Long Hair Custer and his wife would be attending a Strong Heart Dance that the scouts were preparing to host. The scouts donned their best Indian clothing and painted their faces.

They heard the tinkling sound of bells as sleighs arrived outside the scout barracks. Custer stepped down from the first sleigh and held out his hand for his wife. Left Hand wondered if she was sick because she needed a man to help her stand up, but she walked like a healthy younger woman. Custer was a tall man with long red-yellow hair, strong and sinewy. He was not old and fat like the white cooks and the doctor. He had fierce blue eyes and looked like a warrior. His wife was smaller and very pretty. The Indian women held up their babies, and Custer's wife looked at each of them and smiled. She wiggled her fingers at the babies and children. She seemed like a good woman. (5)

The scouts began to dance on the earthen floor near the fireplace while the women sat on their bunks and sang in time to the drum. Left Hand danced the best he could to show his gratitude to Long Hair Custer for the strong gun and the clothing. He was surprised to see a boy about four years old dancing among the warriors. Only warriors did the Strong Heart Dance.

Then came the honoring speeches. A Pȟaláni warrior spoke and a Pȟaláni woman threw a bolt of cloth at his feet and took off her beaded leggings.

"What did he say?" Left Hand asked his wife.

"Her husband and son were killed by a Lakȟóta last year, and this man killed the Lakȟóta who killed them," his wife said. "She honors his revenge with these gifts."

Left Hand kept his face straight. Anger and fighting were forbidden at a Strong Heart Dance. But his stomach burned, and not with hunger.

"Why do they let the little boy dance with the warriors?" he asked. His wife had had Mandan playmates as a child and the Lakȟóta language, which was similar to the Mandan language, came natural to her.

"When they had the fight with the Lakȟóta outside the fort last year, she gave the boy a knife and told him to stick it into a dying Lakȟóta," she said, somewhat embarrassed. "It was his first coup and the warriors said he was a little warrior and could wear an eagle feather now."

Left Hand said nothing. The first man to touch a dying enemy and the man who cut his throat each won the right to wear an eagle feather. But he was not happy.

An old Lakȟóta in a black robe approached to speak. "My son was also a warrior," the old Lakȟóta man said in a quavering voice. "He fought in that fight and killed many Pȟaláni until they killed him at last. He was a great warrior." Then the old man began to weep for his son, and he pulled his black blanket over his head so that no one could see his tears.

A young Pȟaláni jumped up and threw off his robe. "Boast no more of your dead son," the Pȟaláni said in broken Lakȟóta. "It was I who killed him!"

Then he turned to the circle of Pȟaláni warriors. "Will he not fight me? I stand ready!"

Left Hand felt for his belt knife. But his wife touched his hand in warning. Nobody could beat a left-handed man in a knife fight and he knew he could win. But fighting at a Strong Heart dance was forbidden. Even the Pȟaláni knew that a challenge to an old man was cowardly and a disgrace. Some of them showed it with quiet looks of contempt. Left Hand folded his robe over the knife at his belt. If he ever met this cowardly braggart on the open plains, he too would have a coup to count. Long Hair Custer and his wife smiled uneasily and after staying just long enough to deny they were frightened, they left quietly.

"You did right not to fight him," Left Hand's wife said. "He is a barking dog."

"He is a dog whose meat is no good," Left Hand agreed. "This is not a place for killing."

A few days later, Left Hand saw his wife pick up their baby in its cradleboard and duck out with some of the other women, giggling and joking as if they were up to some mischief. Left Hand was proud that his young wife was a one-man woman. Showing jealousy without cause was a sign of weakness or foolishness. But what were these giggling women up to? He followed them, but at a distance, pretending he was headed to look after his horse.

The women were headed for the Custer House like a herd of antelope. Long Back, the wife of the chief of scouts, was in the lead, wearing one of those funny black hats that looked like the end of a cannon barrel. The women began to sing and dance. Left Hand saw his wife, with the baby in the cradle-board, dancing among them. He felt proud of his pretty young wife and of his little daughter. Custer's wife and the other white women came out to watch from the front steps of the house. A black white man who lived with the officers ran out to join the dance. He seemed not to know that the dance was for women only. The women chased him waving a saber and tomahawks and he ran away laughing and escaped. (6) Custer's wife and the other women waved and the Indian woman waved back.

Women made life more cheerful, Left Hand thought. He headed off to look after his horse.

Later that day, Left Hand came back to the Soldier's House and found his wife and some of the other women slicing up fresh beef.

"Did you like our dance?" his wife asked. She knew Left Hand had been watching.

"I was proud of you and of our daughter," Left Hand said. "You were the best woman there and our daughter was the best baby."

"Custer's wife sent us a whole beef," his wife said. "Tonight I brought you food instead of the other way around." They both smiled. She was a good woman and the baby looked more like her by the day.

Left Hand walked down the row of bunks until he saw Running Bear.

"Come to dinner," he asked his friend. "My wife and the women danced up a beef for us."

Running Bear nodded sadly.

"Not hungry?" Left Hand asked his friend, who was now like a younger brother to him. "Are you sick?"

"My heart is heavy from something I heard," Running Bear said.

"May I know of it?" Left Hand asked.

"Son-Of-Star, Bull Head, and Black Fox and some Mandans went to Washington last year to see the white man's chief of Indians," Running Bear said. "He told them that he had made up his mind to fight Sitting Bull, not that year, but not in ten years either, more like two or three. He said that Sitting Bull was like a man in a room locked up by whites, and that he had nowhere to go. He asked for the Pȟaláni and said he would give them guns and pay for any who were killed. He also said that when the fighting was over, the Lakȟóta would have no more land and that the Pȟaláni should treat them well and share with them. But he said the Lakȟóta would be prisoners, like the white men the soldiers keep locked up in the house with iron bars." (7)

Left Hand hid his feelings from his face. His stomach burned.

"Now I have no wish for food either," he said.

(1)   Custer, Elizabeth, BOOTS AND SADDLES, OR LIFE IN DAKOTA WITH GENERAL CUSTER, Harper & Brothers, New York, 1885 (facsimile edition) Page 132

(2)   Libby, Orin, THE ARIKARA NARRATIVE, Page 45

(3)   Ibid, Page 45-46

(4)   Ibid, Page 46

(5)   Custer, BOOTS AND SADDLES, Pages 132-137)

(6)   Ibid, 137

(7)   Libby, Orin, THE ARIKARA NARRATIVE, Pages 38-40

THE BLACK HILLS
GOLD RUSH

Even before the Sioux Treaty of 1868, rumors had percolated to trading posts and frontier settlements that the Black Hills were full of gold—and that the Lakota people would kill any white man who ventured in to dig for it.

In 1863, Frederic Gerard, a French-American trader who lived with the Arikara [Pȟaláni] at Fort Berthold, married to an Arikara woman, met a party of white prospectors with a boatload of gold dust headed down the Missouri River for St. Louis. Gerard tried to warn that them that the Sioux, who had been angered by a punitive action after the Great Sioux Uprising in Minnesota, would be watching the river, and urged them not to take a chance.

The prospectors refused to listen, bought supplies from Gerard, and headed down the river. The prospectors are said to have spotted an elderly Indian fishing on a sandbar. They shot him for target practice. Further down the Missouri, an angry Lakota war party ambushed the boat and killed every man, woman and child on board. Gerard heard about the massacre and sent two Arikaras to search the wrecked boat. They brought back coffee pots and tin cans full of gold dust. The gold probably came from the Montana gold fields that led to Red Cloud's War. But rumors about the Black Hills gold persisted. (1)

After the Lakota, Northern Cheyenne, and Northern Arapaho had fought the Army to a standstill in Red Cloud's War, the Sioux Treaty of 1868 had obligated the Army to keep gold seekers and other settlers out of the Black Hills. In 1873, Custer and the Seventh Cavalry had fought the "Sitting Bull Sioux"—Hunkpapas and young warriors from other Lakota tribes—to prevent the Indians from stopping the advance of the Northern Pacific Railroad into the Yellowstone country. Custer claimed a victory over the Sioux, but the Northern Pacific Railroad collapsed financially during the Panic of 1873. Railroad construction stopped, more for lack of money than fear of Indians. The Panic of 1873 deepened into the worst depression in American history for a number of reasons: more railroads had been built than anybody needed at the time, and in Europe, France retired the bonds used to pay off the Franco-Prussian War ahead of schedule. The bankers and investors in New York and Philadelphia lost two big gilt-edged investments at the same time.

On June 25, 1874, the 10 companies of Custer's Seventh Cavalry, re-united at Fort Abraham Lincoln for the first time in years, was organizing for an expedition to explore the unchartered territory in the western and southwestern portion of Dakota Territory—the Black Hills. The official purpose was an expedition to look for better military roads between Fort Lincoln and Fort Laramie, and to collect scientific information. The expedition would include Professor N.H. Winchell of Minneapolis as a geologist, and two experienced gold prospectors—Horatio Nelson Ross and William T. McKay—to look for any possible gold deposits along the route. Three newspaper reporters eager to report a new gold strike or a new fight with the Indians also tagged along: William Eleroy Curtis of the *Chicago*

Inter-Ocean, Samuel J. Barrows of the *New York Tribune*, and Nathan H. Knappen of the *Bismarck Tribune*.

The departure was delayed because the entire Seventh Cavalry was being re-armed: the Seventh's seven-shot Spencer carbines were replaced with longer-range, single-shot Springfield carbines chambered for powerful 45/55 cartridges. The infantry rifle, known as the Long Tom, was chambered for the even more powerful 45/70 cartridge with a longer range. The accident-prone Remington cap-and-ball revolvers loaded with black powder were replaced with high-quality Colt .45 six-shooters loaded with metal cartridges. The expedition also took along three horse-drawn Gatling machine guns on wheels which could fire 250 rounds per minute, and a three-inch breech-loading rifled cannon that could fire explosive shells a distance of three miles or more. (2)

Two companies of infantry soldiers—Company I of the 20th Infantry and Company G of the 17th Infantry—went along to help with the Gatling guns and artillery. About 60 Indian scouts led by Bloody Knife, more than 100 wagons, and a herd of 300 beef cattle were also part of the expedition, which finally left Fort Abraham Lincoln on July 2.

The ground that the expedition covered for the first two weeks was reported as rugged and poor, with intense heat and little forage or firewood. Private John Cunningham of Company H tried to go on sick leave due to diarrhea, but the medical officer, Captain J. W. Williams, refused to accept him on sick leave and returned him to duty. The next day, Cunningham fell off his horse and was placed in a wagon. (4)

When the Seventh Cavalry reached the outskirts of the Black Hills, Custer and his officers and scientists understood why the Sioux prized the region. The grass was abundant, trees were frequent, and the water in the streams was pure and cool. (3)

On July 21, Private Cunningham died. He was wrapped in canvas and laid in an ambulance—in those days, ambulance was a term for any four-wheeled vehicle. As the troopers saddled the next morning, Private William Roller of M Company settled an argument by shooting Private George Turner in the belly with his Colt 45, in an apparent gunfight. Private Turner was also wrapped in canvas and both troopers were buried at Inyan Creek on July 22 with the regiment lined up for the services. (5)

A few days later, Custer discovered the ashes of an Indian campfire and sent Bloody Knife out to reconnoiter. Bloody Knife located five Indian lodges. Custer took E Company and two Sioux scouts and rode into a camp of 27 Indian men, women, and children. Hands were shaken all around and the Lakota asked Custer for coffee. One Stab, the Lakota sub-chief, came in with four men, ate, and then tried to slip away. A scuffle between an Arikara scout and a Lakota led to a random gunshot, and three of the Lakota got away. The scouts found that while One Stab and his three top warriors were having coffee with Custer, the other Lakota warriors and the women and children had made good their escape. Custer kept One Stab in custody for three days and then released him unharmed. (6)

Custer's two experienced prospectors, Ross and McKay, had been panning wherever they found running water. Some of the troopers copied them, but the troopers found no real traces of gold. The prospectors, however, found gold dust at a sand bar on Harney Creek that could yield 7 cents a pan, and later at Custer Gulch found soil that might yield 10 cents a pan. Ross said he doubted if any of the sites he had prospected would yield more than $50 to $75 a day to an experienced miner. Shortly, however, the three reporters sent out stories that gold had been discovered. One story filled the entire front page of the *Bismarck Tribune* under a headline: "New El Dorado of America." (6)

The expedition broke camp on August 6 for a return march to Fort Lincoln. On the way back, Custer, Bloody Knife, and Captain William Ludlow pumped multiple bullets into a grizzly bear which turned out to be old and scarred with worn-down teeth. The dead bear was posed for a famous photograph. Standing behind Custer, Bloody Knife and Ludlow was Private John Noonan, whose "wife," a Mexican seamstress and laundress known as "Old Nash," later turned out to be a female impersonator. Noonan shortly denied everything, and ultimately committed suicide. (7)

On August 13, Private James King of Company H died after a short, sudden illness. Custer ordered that he be sewn up in canvas and buried that evening. But Colonel Tilford, the commander of the left wing, protested and said that no man of his command would be buried only two hours after being pronounced dead. Victorians had an absolute dread of "premature burial." Custer forged ahead and the left wing stayed behind to bury Private King the next morning.

Disciplinary problems and illnesses began to emerge, and on August 26, Sergeant Charles Sempker of I Company died of chronic diarrhea. When the command reached Fort Abraham Lincoln on August 30 after 60 days in the field, they had covered 1,201 miles. Some of the infantrymen had gunny sacks wrapped around their shoes to hold them together. (8)

Custer's official report disparaged the importance of the actual gold strike. But the telegraph was soon buzzing with orders to Army officers to honor the Sioux Treaty of 1868 and keep prospectors and settlers out of the Black Hills. The miners had been flooding in even before the Black Hills Expedition.

George Herendeen, later a scout for Custer, told the early 20th-Century researcher Walter Mason Camp that on April 5, 1874, he had been one of 149 prospectors who had fought the Lakota and Cheyenne in the Rosebud country of Montana. "We took seven scalps...In the whole expedition we lost one man killed (Zachary Yates) and two wounded." (9) Herendeen said his contingent of illegal prospectors killed 200 Indians but no Lakota remembers anything like this.

"In 1875 we made another expedition with twenty-nine men and had a series of skirmishes with the Indians," Herendeen told Camp, "Five of these were killed and thirteen wounded by end of the season in our various fights. Our expeditions forced the government to open the country, and in 1876 the war started." (10)

Herendeen's casualty count of fallen Indians is highly suspect. But expeditions of prospectors indeed forced the government to begin negotiations to take the Black Hills way from the Lakota and scrap the Sioux Treaty of 1868—the last legal treaty ever signed between the United States and the Sioux. After 1871, treaty-making was discarded and the dealings with Indian tribes were called "agreements."

On September 20, 1875, a special commission chaired by Senator William Allison of Iowa, with General Alfred Terry representing the U.S. Army, met with thousands of unruly but peaceful Indians at White River. Sitting Bull of the Hunkpapas and Crazy Horse, war leader of the independent Oglalas and other western Sioux and their defiant Cheyenne allies, refused to even talk. Red Cloud, regarded as the head chief of all the Sioux, also boycotted the conference. As the commissioners sat under a tarpaulin strung up to provide shade, band after band of young warriors painted for battle and holding guns arrived on horseback. The Lakota formed lines behind the escort of 120 cavalrymen, now heavily outnumbered. Only then, after having shown their power, did the Lakota chiefs arrive to begin discussion.

Senator Allison realized that the Lakota would not give up ownership and their hunting and grazing rights to the Black Hills. He offered them a compromise: "We have now to ask you if you are willing to give our people the right to mine in the Black Hills as long as gold or other valuable minerals are found for a fair and just sum. If you are so willing, we will make a bargain with you for this right. When the gold and other valuable minerals are taken away, the country will again be yours to dispose of in any way you see fit." (11)

Allison added that it would be difficult for the government to keep the white prospectors out of the Black Hills. Red Cloud sent him a messenger asking for a week to discuss the Black Hills with the other senior chiefs. The commissioners gave Red Cloud three days.

Three days later, the commission re-convened. As Red Cloud was about to speak, a young Oglala sub-chief named Little Big Man arrived on horseback leading approximately 300 warriors stripped, painted, and armed for battle. He was an envoy from Chief Crazy Horse.

"I will kill the first chief who speaks for selling the Black Hills," Little Big Man said.

General Terry decided that it was a good time to leave. (12)

A few days later, the commissioners met with 20 senior chiefs at the headquarters building of the Red Cloud Agency. Red Cloud himself did not appear. Spotted Tail, speaking for all the Lakota—or for those who agreed with him—asked the government to submit an offer in writing. The government offered $400,000 a year for the mineral rights to the Black Hills or $6 million for an outright sale, to be paid in installments over the next 40 years. Spotted Tail rejected both offers. Red Cloud had rejected them by his absence. Sitting Bull and Crazy Horse had refused even to talk.

The commissioners returned to Washington and reported that they had failed to convince the Lakota to sell the Black Hills. They suggested that the government unilaterally offer the Sioux a fair price with no consent necessary. The purchase of the land promised to the Lakota in the Sioux Treaty of 1868 "should be presented to them as a finality." (13)

On December 3, 1875, Commissioner of Indian Affairs Edward P. Smith ordered the Indian Agents for the Sioux and Cheyenne to notify all Indians away from their assigned agencies (where many of them received inadequate rations) to report to their agencies by January 31, 1876—the dead of winter, when travel on the Plains was almost impossible and sometimes lethal due to intense cold or snowstorms—or a "military force would be sent to compel them." (14)

(1)   Article, Frederic Francis Gerard (1929—1913) Mandan Historical Society, Mandan, North Dakota, 2006

(2)   Reedstrom, Ernest Lisle, BUGLES, BANNERS AND WAR BONNETS, Bonanza Books, New York, 1986, Pages 84—86

(3)   Ibid, Page 87

(4)   Ibid, Page 87

(5)   Ibid, Page 88

(6)   Ibid, Page 94

(7)   Custer, Elizabeth, BOOTS AND SADDLES, Pages 198—202. Elizabeth Custer, whose marriage was childless, found "Old Nash" affectionate and sympathetic, but wives who had used her services as a midwife shuddered when they learned the truth as they undressed her for burial.

(8)   Reedstrom, Page 97

(9)   Camp, Walter Mason, CUSTER IN '76, Page 220

(10)   Camp, Ibid, Page 220

(11)   Brown, Dee, BURY MY HEARY AT WOUNDED KNEE, Page 282

(12)   Ibid, Page 283

(13)   Ibid, Page 284

(14)   Ibid, Page 285

SIGNING UP MORE SCOUTS

Through the winter at Fort Lincoln, Left Hand and his wife and baby were well fed and had plenty of company. Even his horse had enough food. The Army gave the horses hay or grain to eat all year round, and plenty of it during the snow season when the Indian horses ate dry grass from under the snow or stripped the bark off cottonwood trees. The log house with the big stone fireplace was never cold, even at night, and the Pȟaláni [Arikara] women chattered and played with their children and showed them to the elegant white women who came to visit. The white women wore tight clothes with cloth that shimmered like water and even those who had borne children were skinny in the waist. Left Hand's wife said they did this by lacing in their stomachs with stiff cloth in the way a baby was laced into a Lakȟóta cradleboard, but much tighter. She thought this was strange but admitted that it made the white women look pretty.

Left Hand had learned some Pȟaláni words by listening, but not by asking, so he could follow what people were doing while they talked. He also learned some English words. He never tried to speak either language because most of what he heard was the chatter from the Pȟaláni women: women and men used some different words for the same thing in Lakȟóta.

If a man used woman's words when he talked, he would be teased and asked if we was a *wíŋkte*—a former man who wore a dress and was now a woman—except that it was bad luck to either touch him or to harm him. *Some day I will be able to speak Pȟaláni and English*, Left Hand thought to himself. In the meantime he listened and talked mostly to his wife, who spoke some Lakȟóta, and to Running Bear, who spoke good Lakȟóta and good Pȟaláni and already knew a little English.

When the spring arrived and the snow melted off the fields around the fort, the soldiers started marching again, and it was fun to watch them. The soldiers walked in big groups, all standing straight up, stepping at the same time the way Indian women dance, but the soldiers were not as graceful. Other soldiers in long coats stood to one side with brass things that looked like cannons and played music. Some of them beat drums and some of them played flutes like the Lakȟóta used in courtship. A little man with a bearded face who was their leader waved a little stick at them. The music made Left Hand tap his feet and want to dance.

The Pȟaláni scouts hunted; Left Hand rode with them. When they found game—deer or antelope—they gave some to their wives, some to the white cooks who were afraid of Indians (to keep them friendly), and the rest to those who had no luck.

Left Hand learned that the white men called Bear Running In The Timber "Cards" instead of Running Bear because he loved to play cards with the white men. He usually won. The Pȟaláni called him "Caroo," which is how they pronounced Cards. Running Bear said it was easy to beat the white men at cards because you could always tell what they were thinking. Their eyes betrayed them. Left Hand and Running Bear became friends like an uncle and a nephew. Left Hand also became friendly with Matȟó-ská, White Bear, another Lakȟóta scout, a quiet man who enjoyed good food, and with Maȟpíya-ská, White Cloud, who was sharp and a good horseman. There were four Lakȟóta scouts—the lucky number, because there are four directions and four seasons and all the animals that can think have four limbs.

One day Left Hand saw a number of Pȟaláni he had not seen before lined up at the headquarters building. He nodded to White Cloud and White Bear. Running Bear was off somewhere playing cards.

"The soldier chiefs want more scouts," White Cloud said. "Cards told us that Custer sent a letter to Son-Of-The-Star, the Pȟaláni head chief. He said they needed more scouts. These just came in from Fort Berthold." (1)

Left Hand nodded. They both remembered what Cards had said the Washington chiefs told the Pȟaláni chiefs. Left Hand felt queasy in his stomach.

"Bull Head will no longer be chief of the scouts," White Cloud added. "Here is the story my wife told me. Bull Head said that he was in a fight with the Lakȟóta when they were stealing Pȟaláni horses. The Pȟaláni named Soldier and the white-talker Beauchamp (2), rode with him. The Lakȟóta who stole the horses ran from them but it was a trap. The Lakȟóta horses were fast and out-ran them and then Sitting Bull's band rode in behind them and attacked the fort. Bull Head was thrown from his horse and lay in the grass. Many Pȟaláni saw this. A soldier was about to shoot at the Lakȟóta but Two Chief called to him not to fire. Two Lakȟóta rode up and stood their horses on either side of Bull Head. One of them said 'I am Sitting Bull, himself!' They stood over Bull Head and another Lakȟóta took his gun and his war gear, but did not kill him because of Sitting Bull.

"The white soldiers sent a wagon out to bring Bull Head back later that day. The soldiers and the Pȟaláni all thought he was dead. Then they saw someone coming in over the hill, staggering, hardly able to walk. It was Bull Head. I have heard that Bull Head and Sitting Bull belonged to the same secret society. (3) Bull Head cannot fight a man who saved his life."

Left Hand nodded. "Who will be the new chief of the scouts?" he asked.

"Bloody Knife is Long Hair's friend," White Bear said. "Long Hair trusts his word."

Left Hand shook his head slightly. "Bloody Knife's father is Lakȟóta. The Pȟaláni will want a Pȟaláni as their chief." Then Left Hand remembered he was talking to a scout with more experience and said, "...that is what I think."

"Héčhetu weló, that is right," White Cloud said thoughtfully. "The Pȟaláni say that they are great fighters and that the whites need red men to fight other red men. I heard that in my father's time the whites made war on the Pȟaláni after the Pȟaláni robbed some fur traders. The white soldiers had to ask the Lakȟóta for warriors to help them. If the whites fought the Pȟaláni without the Lakȟóta, they would never be able to beat them even if they could find them." (4)

"The best thing about the whites is the food," Left Hand said with a sigh. He felt sad at heart, but not as sad as he had felt when his wife and daughter were always hungry and he was afraid for his daughter's life. But Left Hand was restless and angry and it was hard to go back to sleep when he awoke after dreaming about his Húŋkpapȟa people at home.

When the weather was warm and the ground was wet with spots of green grass, the scouts were told to meet at Custer's tent by the river. Custer had been away a long time, in Washington, and now he was back and had something to tell the scouts. Cards and Left Hand went. Cards, who understood Pȟaláni, whispered to Left Hand what Custer was saying. Fred Gerard, the white man with the blue eyes and the big beard, translated for Custer to the Pȟaláni. Left Hand thought Custer looked tense and angry, but not angry at the

Indians. *He must have had trouble in Washington,* Left Hand thought.

"The man before me, Bob-tailed Bull, is a man of good heart, of good character," Gerard said for Custer in Pȟaláni as Custer spoke English. "I am pleased to have him here. I am glad he has enlisted. It will be a hard expedition but we will all share the same hardships. I am very well pleased to have him in my party and I told it in Washington. We are to live together and fight together, children of one father and one mother.

"The Great-Grandfather has a plan. The Sioux camps have united and you and I must work together for the Great Father and help each other. The Great Father is well pleased that it was so easy to get Son-of-the-Star to furnish me scouts for this work we have to do and he is pleased, too, in his behavior at helping on the plan of the Great Father. I, for one, am willing to help in this all I can, and you must help too. It is this way, my brothers. If I should happen to lose any of the men Son-of-the-Star has furnished, their reward will not be forgotten by the government. Their relations will be saddened by their death but there will be some comfort in the pay that the United States government will provide." (5)

Bob-tailed Bull spoke. He was a tall, dark man, the chief of the Pȟaláni camp police, slender and strong, with a big fleshy mouth. He wore a beautiful elk skin war shirt embroidered with beadwork.

"It is a good thing you say, my brother, "Bob-tailed Bull said. "My children and other relatives will receive my pay and other rewards. I am glad you say this because I see there is some gain even though I lose my life." (6) The Pȟaláni all grunted an agreement to show they were brave and not afraid to die.

"No more words need be said," Custer said, with Fred Gerard translating. "Bob-tailed Bull is to be the leader and Soldier second in command of the scouts." (7)

Custer gestured and Gerard handed Bob-Tailed Bull a long blue soldier coat with gold strips on the front. This was the sort of coat the bandsmen wore when they stood up and played their music while the little man with the beard waved a little stick at them. Gerard also gave Soldier a bandsman's coat. Bob-tailed Bull looked and saw he had three stripes on the sleeve and Soldier had two stripes. They were happy with themselves.

"Speech," Custer said to Bob-tailed Bull with a smile.

"I am not a man to change tribes all the time; I have always been an Pȟaláni and respected their chiefs and served them gladly," Bob-tailed Bull said. Bloody

Knife glared at him but you had to know Bloody Knife to see it. Left Hand knew that Bloody Knife has been passed over for chief of scouts because his father was Lakȟóta. Left Hand also knew that Bloody Knife had been his true friend and he felt resentful of the slur. *I will show him I am a true friend and not a man to forget his help*, Left Hand thought to himself.

"Yes, Long Hair, I am a member of the police and also a chief. With one hand I hold the position of police among my people and with the other I hold the position of chief of the scouts." (8)

We all know this now, Left Hand thought wryly. Bloody Knife looked sullen.

"My brother—I am going to address you so, for you said we were brothers—I have had experience fighting the Sioux, and when we meet them we shall see each other's bravery." (9)

Custer told the scouts not to leave Fort Lincoln because they would be marching soon. Left Hand started to think. He had given his word to serve for six months. He had one payday left. When he was paid the next time, he would not serve again. He would find a way to warn the Húŋkpapȟa that Custer's soldiers and the Pȟaláni were coming against them. Meanwhile, he would give his wife the greenbacks and bring her and the baby back to her own people. He would join her later and take her back to the Húŋkpapȟa. But he would tell no one of this—not Bloody Knife, and not even Cards.

A few days later, Bloody Knife and some of the other Pȟaláni leaders were asked to meet Custer. Custer was pleased to see Bloody Knife and gave him a medal he brought from Washington. When Custer saw Black Fox, another Pȟaláni scout, he teased him as Indians do: "If he repeats his trick of last time, I will have a remedy; if he takes his wife along again he will be well punished." (10)

He also praised Bob-tailed Bull's beautiful embroidered shirt.

Custer told the Pȟaláni scouts that he had been to Washington and that he had been informed that this would be his last campaign in the West among the Indians. He said that no matter how small a victory he could win, even though it was against only five lodges of Lakȟóta, it would make him President—Great Father—and he must turn back as soon as he was victorious. In case of victory he would take Bloody Knife to Washington. (11)

(1)   Libby, THE ARIKARA NARRATIVE, Page 51

(2)   White-Talker, iyÁ-ská in Lakota, can be used to mean a half-breed because most mixed-blood children learned English or French from their white fathers. Traditional Lakota avoided incest and *wíŋkte*, but had no objection to interracial marriage until they observed that white husbands, especially Army officers, usually deserted their Indian wives.

(3)   Libby, Pages 47—48, THE ARIKARA NARRATIVE, The Arikara scout Soldier, who saw this happen, recounted the story to Orin Libby many years later.

(4)   SOLDIER AND BRAVE, Page 6-7 The first battle between U.S. soldiers and Plains warriors was in 1823, when General Henry Leavenworth led 220 regulars, 120 mountain men, and 400 to 500 Sioux against a smaller force of Arikaras. The National Park Service account reports that the fight "inspired the Arikaras with contempt for the prowess of white men."

(5)   Libby, THE ARIKARA NARRATIVE, Pages 55-56

(6)   Ibid, Page 56

(7)   Ibid, Page 56

(8)   Ibid, Page 57

(9)   Ibid, Page 57

(10)   Ibid, Page 58

(11)   Ibid, Page 58. The account by Red Star is said to be the only source for the idea that Custer planned to run for President. Most historians do not accept Custer's presidential ambitions as factual.

TROUBLE IN WASHINGTON

Custer's agitation, his near-frantic politicking with the Arikara [Pȟaláni] scouts, and his fence-mending with Bloody Knife had a simple explanation: he needed a victory against the Sioux to save his career from an excess of his own headstrong courage and honesty.

Custer had received a telegraphic summons to Washington on March 16, 1876, to testify about charges against the recently resigned Secretary of War, William Worth Belknap, who was accused of presiding over widespread dishonesty in the distribution of post traderships serving Army posts in the West. (1) Since 1870, the War Department had the exclusive right to appoint post traders who ran general stores on Army posts. Before this time, the officers at the post had elected their own sutlers, or store-keepers, who were often retired officers or sergeants who needed a job.

The post tradership scandals began brewing shortly after William Worth Belknap took over as U.S. Secretary of War in Grant's cabinet in 1869. Belknap, the son of an Army general, was a graduate of Princeton and had been trained as a lawyer. He had been a courageous soldier in the Civil War.

"Major Belknap was always in the right place at the right time, encouraging and directing officers and men as coolly as a veteran," his colonel in the 15th Iowa Infantry, H.T Reid, wrote. (2) At the battle of Atlanta in 1864, Belknap leaped over an earthwork and captured a Confederate colonel with one hand and a Confederate private with the other. (3)

Colonel William Hall said Belknap displayed "at all times the highest qualities of a soldier, cheering his men by his voice, and encouraging them with his personal disregard for danger." (4) At the end of the war Belknap was a major general of volunteers. He left the Army after the Civil War to pursue politics. His first wife Cora Le Roy had died in 1862, and after the war Belknap married Carita Tomlinson, a Kentucky belle who had been loyal to the Union. They had a child, but Carita died in 1870, and her widowed sister Amanda moved in to take care of the baby—and Belknap's financial career. (5)

Sometime in 1870, either Carita or Amanda Tomlinson (soon to be Belknap) approached a friend of the family, Caleb Marsh, and told him that she had a perfect investment idea: a post tradership. Marsh knew nothing about Indians and was probably afraid of them, but he filled out an application on August 16, 1870 and received a War Department appointment as post trader of Fort Sill, Indian Territory (now Oklahoma).

The trader at Fort Sill, John S. Evans, wanted to keep his lucrative monopoly for supplying officers, officers' and soldiers' wives and troopers with everything from soap and canned food to whiskey and tobacco. Marsh and Evans cut a deal: Evans would send Marsh $12,000 a year and keep whatever else he earned supplying the soldiers and their families. The results were soon apparent to the soldiers.

"Why, those fellows had things so that you couldn't buy anything at the posts without getting it from them," Sergeant Daniel Kanipe of Custer's 7th Cavalry recalled in 1924. "Liquor was 25 cents a glass and the glasses was mostly glass—mighty little whiskey. Custer set a maximum price and it caused his arrest [sic] But all the high army officers were with him and he was given a command at the place I spoke of." (6)

Custer, himself a teetotaler since 1864, was not actually arrested because he set a fixed price for post trader whisky. But Custer had endorsed Othniel Marsh as a disinterested witness in the Indian Department food scandal. Custer had also objected in writing when the post trader at Fort Abraham Lincoln had tried to enforce a monopoly on the sale of broad-brimmed campaign hats for troopers. The post trader had objected when General Custer's younger brother, Tom Custer, had bought better hats cheaper off-post. The protests from Custer and other frontier officers were duly noted but not much happened—except that William and Amanda Belknap maintained one of the most elegant and luxurious households in Washington with an English butler, a French maid, 40 pairs of shoes, and a wedding trousseau from Charles Frederic Worth of Paris that cost $6,000, all out of Belknap's official salary of $8,000.

Caleb Marsh was not the only investor who loved post traderships. Orvil Grant, the president's brother, owned a piece of three trading posts, and the president's brother-in-law owned another trading post under President Grant's own signatures. William Tomlinson, Carita and Amanda's brother, owned one too—and he was the only former Confederate officer to become a post trader. (7)

Elizabeth Custer noted that besides selling overpriced merchandise to officers, soldiers, and Army wives, the government-licensed traders sold guns to the Indians. "We even saw on a steamer touching at our landing, its freight of Springfield rifles piled up on the decks en route for the Indians up the river. There was unquestionable proof that they came into the trading posts far above us and bought them, while our own brave 7th Cavalry troopers were sent out with only short-range carbines that grew foul after the second firing." (8)

William and Amanda Belknap's world of luxurious elegance started to collapse when the dinosaur-hunter Othniel Marsh dropped off the samples of tainted food that Red Cloud had given him in Washington. The New York Herald, the leading Democratic newspaper, began to expand its commentary by noting that "vague rumors had reached the capital" that post traders had to pay a "tax" on their profits in the form of a kick-back to the Secretary of War.

On March 1, 1876, Hiester Clymer, Belknap's former roommate at Princeton, but now chairman of the U.S. House Committee on Expenditures in the War Department, sent a message to Belknap telling him that he wanted to discuss testimony they had heard from a certain Caleb Marsh. Congressman Clymer also advised his former roommate William Worth Belknap to resign immediately to keep from being sent to prison for two years for accepting bribes.

On March 2, Belknap was literally on his knees before an astounded President Grant begging Grant to immediately accept his resignation. Grant wrote a letter of acceptance to Belknap, who was now in tears. That same day, Belknap—now the former Secretary of War—was impeached by the U.S. House of Representatives. A lawyer himself, Belknap hired a lawyer of his own, Montgomery Blair. When Belknap appeared before the House he said: "Some things are true, some things are not true, and some things I know nothing about. . . . Only grant my wish that this investigation shall be pursued no further as affecting any member of my family." (9)

The Congressmen who were to hear the impeachment were not hostile to Belknap: Hiester Clymer was one of his oldest friends. Kentucky Congressman Joseph Blackburn's wife had been a friend of

Amanda Belknap since childhood and Lorenzo Danforth was a lawyer-politician from Ohio and also a Civil War veteran like Belknap. (10)

The Belknap family, however, was taking no chances. Amanda and her brother William, who owned a post tradership himself, cornered Caleb Marsh and tried to make him sign a statement that Belknap himself had been innocent and only Carita and Amanda— who were not federal officials and not liable to charges of accepting bribes—had handled the money. Caleb Marsh wrote a wishy-washy letter that seemed to exonerate Belknap himself but he told a different story before the House Committee: He said he gave some of the money directly to Belknap. "The money was sent according to the instructions of the secretary of war: sometimes in bank notes by Adams' Express...Usually, when I sent money by express, I would send him the receipt of the company which he would either return marked 'OK' or otherwise acknowledge the receipt of the same. Sometimes I paid him in person in New York, when his receipt was necessary."

Custer appeared before the House Committee at the end of March and told how he and his brother Tom had tried to buy better campaign hats at lower prices from a merchant in St. Paul until the post trader at Fort Abraham Lincoln, R.C. Seip, made a written complaint to Belknap to protect his guaranteed monopoly "claiming that under the privilege he held as trader, nobody, no officer even, had the right to buy anything elsewhere or bring it there, but must buy everything through him."

Custer then provided a copy of the letter that Belknap had written to him dated December 1, 1874. "The [traders] will be allowed the exclusive privilege of trade upon the military reserve to which they are appointed, and no other person will be allowed to trade, peddle, or sell goods, by sample or otherwise, within the limits of the reserve. That clause is plain, clear and explicit and means what it says. In the opinion of the secretary of war, these circulars are clear enough for anyone to understand who deserves to do so and he has only to repeat the statement made many times that 'any violation of either of these circumstances . . . will be promptly acted upon.'" (11)

Custer, who had once tracked down some citizens stealing oats from the Army, leaned on Seip and got him to admit that a massive kick-back scheme existed but that Seip himself did not know where the money ended up. Seip admitted that he paid two men named Rice and Hedrick, two of Belknap's political cronies in Iowa. "He said he knew positively only that he paid to Rice and Hedrick, but he was always under the impression that a portion of it went to the secretary of war."

Custer also remembered that President Grant's brother Orvil had shown up at Fort Lincoln and that Custer had reluctantly loaned Orvil an ambulance—an Army passenger wagon—to visit his own investments. "I told him I would not give it to him as a trader, but that to any member of the president's family visiting there, out of courtesy to the president of the United States, I would render any facility I could." (12)

Grant was livid. He himself knew that his brother and former business partner Orvil had repeatedly been charged with dishonesty and graft. (13) But Grant's desire to protect his own family, right or wrong, turned into a rage against Custer. He refused to allow Custer to leave Washington and indicated that somebody else would have to command the expedition against the Sioux that summer.

Custer attempted to see Grant but he was denied an interview. Custer attempted to see General Sherman, but missed him at his office. Custer then attempted to see Grant again. On May 4, denied an interview with Grant, Custer took the night train from Washington to Chicago. When Custer got off the train in Chicago on May 5, he was placed under military arrest. President Grant had now definitely decided that

Custer was not to command the expedition against the Sioux.

Democratic newspapers castigated Grant as a corrupt tyrant and extolled Custer as a hero—which only made Grant angrier. Custer's last appeal was to General Alfred Terry. General Terry interceded for Custer and at the last minute, Sheridan also interceded. Custer was granted tactical command of the 7th Cavalry with the approval of General Sherman and General Sheridan.

"... General Custer's urgent request to go under your command with his regiment has been submitted to the President, who sent me word that if you want General Custer along he withdraws his objections," Sherman telegrammed to Terry on May 8. "Advise Custer to be prudent, not to take along any newspaper men, who always make mischief, and to abstain from personalities in the future. . . . W.T. Sherman, General" (14)

Belknap was eventually acquitted, but only on a technicality. Of the members of the U.S. Senate who tried him, 35 Senators voted "guilty" and 25 voted "not guilty"—but 22 said that they voted "not guilty" only because they believed that Belknap could not be convicted once he had resigned. In the years to come, the Clymer commission would be forgotten: when Hiester

Clymer died of apoplexy in 1884, the New York Times never mentioned the Belknap impeachment and some of the local newspapers spelled Clymer's first name wrong. (15) But when Custer spoke to the Arikara scouts and to Bloody Knife at Fort Abraham Lincoln, he knew he needed a victory—not to be elected president, but simply to keep his position in the Army.

(1)   Libby, THE ARIKARA NARRATIVE. Pages 57-58

(2)   Dictionary of American Biography, Volume II, Page 148.

(3)   ENCYCLOPEDIA OF THE AMERICAN CIVIL WAR, Volume 1, Page 204, article by Kenneth L. Lyftogt (CQ)

(4)   DICTIONARY OF AMERICAN BIOGRAPHY, Volume II, Page 148

(5)   The information about the Belknap Scandal is recorded in federal publications now almost impossible to find, but encapsulated in "The Belknap Scandal: Fulcrum To Disaster", *Wild West* magazine, June 2010, by John Koster, based on those documents.

(6)   Graham, W.A., THE CUSTER MYTH, Page 248, citing a newspaper story from the Greensboro, N.C. Daily Record of April 27, 1924.

(7)   *Wild West* magazine, THE BELKNAP SCANDAL, Page 60

(8)   Custer, Elizabeth, BOOTS AND SADDLES, Page 266

(9)   WILD WEST, THE BELKNAP SCANDAL, Page 61

(10)   Ibid, Page 61

(11)   Ibid, Page 63, also quoted in Dr. Charles Kuhlman's LEGEND INTO HISTORY, now out of print.

(12)   Ibid, Page 64

(13)   McFeeley, GRANT: A BIOGRAPHY, W.W. Norton & Company, New York and London, 1981. Pages 413, 430

(14)   Reedstrom, Ernest Lisle, BUGLES, BANNERS AND WAR BONNETS, Page 109

(15)   *The New York Times*, June 13, 1884, Hiester Clymer obituary.

DEATH SONG
ON HORSEBACK

On March 17, at 7 a.m., the 7th Cavalry marched from Fort Abraham Lincoln against the Sioux. The company of Pȟaláni [Arikara] scouts led the way with a parade. Frederic Gerard, the scout and interpreter with the blue eyes and the big beard, told the Pȟaláni that they should assemble by warrior societies: The New Dog Society, the oldest warriors, led the way. The Grass Dance Society followed, led by Bob-tailed Bull and Young Hawk, another experienced Pȟaláni who had wanted to stay home until his father pledged him to

89

Custer. The Da-roch'-pa Society came last, and the four Lakȟóta scouts followed on their own: Bear Running In The Timber, almost always known as Cards, (Caroo), White Bear (Matȟó-ská), White Cloud (Maȟpíya-ská) and Left Hand. (1)

"Some of these soldiers can barely stay on their horses," Cards said. "Their eyes show fear. This will end badly for them."

"It could end badly for us too," White Cloud said. "We should sing our Death Song."

"Good," said Left Hand. Cards and White Bear nodded and they all took a deep breath and began to sing in high, quavering Lakȟóta, because this was spirit music for the people in the next world to hear too.

"The young man who did not come home,
"He died in the middle of his enemies
"He was a Lakȟóta warrior!
"This is what he was born for!"

Elizabeth Custer heard the singing with foreboding. ". . . weird and melancholy beyond description," she wrote 10 years later. "Their war-song is misnamed when called music. It is more of a lament or a dirge than an inspiration to activity. This intonation they kept up for miles along the road." (2)

Left Hand saw his wife holding up the baby in her cradleboard to look at him. He nodded and she nodded back. Inside the cradleboard she had stitched most of the greenbacks the Army had paid him since he enlisted. He had told her that she should go home to her people and help them with the money. Some of the other scouts' wives would also be going back to Fort Berthold. She would be safe there and he would come back to her if he lived. White men had a hard time telling Indian women from younger Indian men, and telling man from man or woman from woman was completely beyond them. Anyway, she was Pȟaláni and her own tribe would keep the whites from hurting her.

"After we had passed the Indian quarters we came near Laundress Row, and there my heart entirely failed me," Elizabeth Custer remembered. "The wives and children of the soldiers lined the road. Mothers, with streaming eyes, held their little ones out at arm's-length for one last look at their departing fathers...Unfettered by conventional restrictions, and indifferent to the opinions of others, the grief of these women was audible, and was accompanied by desponding gestures, dictated by their bursting hearts and expressions of their abandoned grief." (3)

Elizabeth Custer rode beside her husband for the first day of the march, but most of the officers' wives had stayed indoors and watched from the latticed windows. The band played "The Girl I left Behind Me." (4)

The column included the Indian scouts, twelve companies of cavalry, a platoon of Gatling guns with two officers and 32 infantrymen, a herd of cattle for beef, dozens of pack mules, and about 150 wheeled vehicles. This was part of the biggest U.S. military expedition since the Civil War had ended 11 years before.

The soldiers were paid off when they came for the first night, at the Heart River. The soldiers grumbled because there was nothing to buy—Bloody Knife told the four Lakȟóta scouts with his snide smile that Custer knew if the white soldiers had their pay before they left, many would get too drunk to ride and some would run away. Elizabeth Custer and Custer's sister Margaret Calhoun returned to Fort Lincoln the next day with the paymaster.

Some of the Pȟaláni scouts hunted while they were riding on the sides of the column, and sold the wild game to the soldiers. They got wonderful prices— the soldiers were free with their money. They ate fresh meat and threw away their hardtack on the trail.

One night Custer called the scouts together. Bloody Knife was standing next to Custer and Frederic Gerard was the interpreter. Custer told them that he had been to Washington and had been told to follow the Lakȟóta, and that he must have a victory. "When we return, I will go back to Washington, and on my trip to Washington I shall take my brother here, Bloody Knife, with me.

"I shall remain in Washington and be the Great Father. But my brother, Bloody Knife, will return and when he arrives home he will have a fine house built for him, and those of you present will be the ones appointed to look after the work that will be placed in Bloody Knife's charge. You will have positions under him to help in what he is to do and you can, when you wish to speak to me or send me word, gather at Bloody Knife's house and decide what that message will be. Then he will send it to me. He will be given the whole tribe of the Pȟaláni to be head of. I will have papers made out for each of you, and you will have plenty to eat for all times to come, and your children.

"When these papers are in your hands, you will have food to eat always. In case your child is hungry and wants something to eat, take your papers to any citizen and he will divide with you. Take them to any store, and when they are read, they will speak and tell what you wish and you will get it. You will be the ones after we return who have charge of the Pȟaláni tribe." (5)

The four Lakȟóta scouts said among themselves that now Custer seemed to trust Bloody Knife more than Bob-tailed Bull, perhaps because Bloody Knife was half Lakȟóta and spoke both languages well, or perhaps because Custer had known Bloody Knife a long time. Bob-tailed Bull looked dark in the face inside his fancy blue bandsman's coat with the yellow stripes.

On the eighth night, Custer detailed two Pȟaláni scouts, One Horn and Red Foolish Bear, to take the mail back to Fort Lincoln. John Howard was the interpreter at the post in place of Frederic Gerard. He gave One Horn and Foolish Red Bear the mail, and the Pȟaláni women loaded them down with spare moccasins for their husbands. The scouts could follow the soldiers' trail by the hardtack and other food the soldiers had thrown away. Red Foolish Bear's horse gave out on the way back, but Bob-tailed Bull and some of the other scouts came out and found him afoot. They brought him breakfast and a fresh horse. (6)

At Camp 11, the scouts had a horse race between the Pȟaláni scout, Stabbed, and the Lakȟóta scout, Buffalo Cow Father, with each side betting $10. The next day, the regiment reached the Dakȟóta Badlands and Custer ordered no shooting. Bob Jackson, a half-blood Blackfoot scout, spotted a rattlesnake in the river and shot at it with a revolver. Jackson was placed under discipline, which meant that he had to stand on top of a barrel balancing on one foot. (7)

The 7th Cavalry now crossed the Little Missouri River at Sentinel Butte. This was Camp 13. As an unseasonal snowstorm approached, Custer decided that he would send scouts back with replies to the mail that the first scouts had brought in.

"It has been decided to send scouts back to Lincoln," Custer wrote to his wife. "They leave here at daylight and will remain there thirty-six hours, returning to us with dispatches and mail.

"The scouts that were left at Lincoln joined us yesterday about 10 A.M. with the mail. . . ." Custer added. "I wish that you knew how good it was to get the letters. You must send me more by the scouts we send out tomorrow. . . . Since beginning this letter it is decided that they go at once, for I know it is best to get them out of camp at night; so they have been directed to saddle-up immediately, and I must therefore cut this letter short." (8)

The scouts sent back with the mail were the Phaláni, Scabby Wolf, and the Lakȟóta, Left Hand. (9)

(1)   Libby, THE ARIKARA NARRATIVE, Page 59. Red Star, an Arikara scout, mentions four Lakota scouts: One of these scouts was Caroo, (Cards), another was Matȟó-ská (White Bear or Bear Who Waits), a third was Maȟpíya-ská (White Cloud), the fourth was Pté-até (Buffalo Ancestor). Red Star also mentions that Left Hand was sent back with Custer's mail from Camp 13 and returned a few days later. Walter Mason Camp in "Custer In '76" (Page 287) lists five Sioux scouts with Custer in 1876: Broken Penis, also called Kanept in Arikara or Growling Bear in English; Cards, also called Karu or Caroo, whose Indian name, Bear Running In The Timber, was not listed; Left Hand, also called Qhci in Arikara— Napé Čhatká is Left Hand in Lakota; Sticking Out; and Shield, called Waháčhaŋka in Lakota. Since all Indian sources report four Lakota scouts, and Buffalo Ancestor (Pté-até) is not on Camp's Army list but Left Hand is, Buffalo Ancestor may have been Left Hand. Many Indians were known by more than one name at the same time.

(2)   Custer, Elizabeth, BOOTS AND SADDLES, Page 262

(3)   Ibid, Page 262 - 263

(4)   Graham. W.A., in THE CUSTER MYTH, Page 125, from the 1921 version of 'The Godfrey Narrative,' originally published in *Century* magazine in 1892.

(5)   Libby, THE ARIKARA NARRATIVE, Pages 62—63. NB —while historian Mari Sandoz believed Custer planned to run for president, he may have been using the term Great Father for some other important government position.

(6)   Ibid, Pages 63-65

(7)   Ibid, Pages 66 -67

(8)   Custer, Elizabeth, BOOTS AND SADDLES, Pages 304-305

(9)   Libby, Orin, THE ARIKARA NARRATIVE, Page 67

BAD MEDICINE ROAD

Left Hand and Scabby Wolf, the Arikara [Pȟa-láni], came back from the mail delivery as the snow was melting into slush and vanishing. The command had waited for four days. (1) The soldiers began to move faster into Sioux country. Now Custer detailed three Arikara scouts—the teenaged Young Hawk and his father Forked Horn, One Feather, and the experienced Lakota scout, Cards, to join a cavalry patrol up the Powder River. Running Wolf, another Arikara, said separately that four Lakota scouts were sent on this patrol: "Caroo, Matȟó-ská, Buffalo Body (Pté-até, actually Buffalo Ancestor) and White Cloud." Left Hand is not named and this may be after he left the command. Or Left Hand may also have been called Buffalo Body or Buffalo Father. The Arikara Young Hawk, an energetic teenager eager for his father's approval, rode up a hill and spotted the remnants of an abandoned Lakota camp in the distance. The scouts and soldiers found and counted spaces for about 350 lodges. (2)

The next day, the scouts followed an old Lakota pony trail and found a shallow entrenchment. The scouts said that a number of white men had fought and been killed. The soldiers believed this had been a party of prospectors who had trespassed into the Sioux treaty lands after the Black Hills gold strike and had been wiped out. (3)

"What do you think of this trail, Forked Horn?" Major Marcus Reno, the commander of the reconnaissance party, asked the oldest Arikara scout.

"If the Dakȟótas see us, the sun will not move very far before we are all killed," Forked Horn replied. "But you are the leader and we will go on if you say so."

"Custer told us to turn back if we found the trail, and we will return, these are our orders," Reno said, according to the Arikara scouts. (4) The scouting party turned and followed the Rosebud River down to the Elk

River and found Custer's camp. The wagons had all been left at the Powder River under guard of the infantry soldiers, but the Arikara found a white man in a tent selling liquor. The Indians reported that the soldiers around the tent looked like a swarm of flies. The scouts were forbidden to drink until Frederic Gerard said that they could have one drink each. Custer now had some idea where the Lakota camp would be. He prepared to go into action. The Arikara were told that if the command broke up, they were to return to the campsite.

Two days later, the command reached a Lakota camp that had been abandoned the winter before. "I was at the head of the column and as we rode through . . . suddenly came upon a human skull lying under the remains of an extinct fire," Custer wrote to Elizabeth. "I halted to examine and lying near by I found the uniform of a soldier. Evidently it was a cavalry uniform. As the buttons on the overcoat had a 'C' on them, and the dress-coat had the yellow cord of the cavalry running through it. The skull was weatherbeaten and had evidently been there several months. All the circumstances went to show that the skull was that of some poor mortal who had been a prisoner in the hands of the savages, and who doubtless had been tortured to death, probably burned . . ."(5)

Custer stood there some time and looked down at the remains of the soldier, Red Star noted.

The command also found a Lakota burial scaffold with the uprights painted red and black—the birth-and-death marks of a brave warrior. Custer didn't tell his wife this part, but he had the warrior's body looted of its finery and thrown into the river. (6) The Arikara, however, saw that the dead warrior had a partially healed gunshot wound just below the right shoulder. No one understood that this warrior had almost certainly been fatally wounded in the battle with General George Crook's command at the Rosebud on June 17—a battle that Custer never heard about. Crook fought the Lakota and Cheyenne to a stalemate on June 17 with the help of his Crow and Shoshone scouts. But in the end it was Crook, with a command far bigger than Custer's, who gave up the field and retreated back toward his base.

Custer now had some Crow scouts of his own he had purchased from Colonel John Gibbon, who was leading the third and smallest element of the three units sent to surround the Lakota.

". . . they are familiar with the country," Custer wrote in his last letter to Elizabeth on June 21. "They are magnificent-looking men, so much handsomer and more Indian-like than any we have ever seen, and so jolly and sportive; nothing of the gloomy, silent red-man about them. They have formally given themselves to me, after the usual talk. In their speech they said they had heard that I never abandon a trail; that when my food gave out I ate mule. That was the kind of man they wanted to fight under; they were willing to eat mule too." (7)

Custer conferred with General Terry on the steamer *Far West*, and told his officers he intended to follow the trail until he could get the Indians—even if he had to chase them—to their assigned agencies on the Missouri River or the border of Nebraska. The ammunition and food was shifted from the steamboat and wagons to pack mules, better able to keep up with the cavalry and scouts. Each soldier was issued 100 rounds of carbine ammunition and 24 rounds of pistol ammunition, and the pack mules were loaded with 50 more rounds of carbine ammunition per man, 15 days rations of hardtack and coffee, and 12 days rations of bacon. Custer told the men to take extra salt in case they had to live on horse meat. (8) The Gatling guns, however, were left with General Terry because their wheeled carriages might slow up the command on broken ground.

"Here Gerard told us he wanted us to sing our death songs," the Arikara Red Star said. "... Custer had a heart like an Indian; if we ever left one thing out of our ceremonies he always suggested it to us. We got on our horses and rode around singing the songs. . . . At supper, Bloody Knife was missing, and the scouts waited for him until it was late but he was drunk somewhere; he got liquor from somebody. Next morning at breakfast Bloody Knife appeared leading a horse . . ." (9)

Toward nightfall, the Custer command reached the grounds for a Sun Dance, the most important ritual of the Lakota. After purifying themselves with sweat baths in steam made by pouring water over heated rocks, the Lakota danced to exhaustion or offered pieces of their own flesh in the hope of obtaining spiritual powers.

"Here was evidence of the Dakȟótas [Lakȟóta] having made medicine, the sand had been arranged and smoothed, and pictures had been drawn," Red Bear said. "The Dakȟóta scouts in Custer's army said this meant the enemy knew that the army was coming." In one of the sweat lodges was a long heap or ridge of sand. On this one Red Bear, Red Star, and Soldier saw figures drawn indicating by hoof prints Custer's men on one side and the Dakota on the other. Between them dead men were drawn lying with their heads toward the Dakotas. The Arikara scouts understood this to mean that the Dakota medicine was too strong for them and they would be defeated by the Dakotas. . . .

"On the right bank of the Rosebud as they marched they saw Dakota inscriptions on the sandstone of the hills on their left. One of these inscriptions showed two buffalo fighting, and various interpretations were given by the Arikara as to the meaning of these figures . . . All the Arikara knew what this meant, that the Dakota were sure of winning." (10)

Late in the day on June 24, Custer sent for the white leader of the scouts, Lieutenant Charles Varnum, a West Pointer and veteran of the Yellowstone and Black Hills Expeditions. Custer was not happy.

"The command halted and I was sent for and came back to the head of the column," Varnum wrote to Walter Mason Camp in 1909. "Custer told me that [Edward S.] Godfrey had reported that a trail of a part of the Indians had gone up a branch stream trail to our left about ten miles back and Custer was rather angry that I had let anything get away from me. I told him of the thoroughness of my work at the front where I had the two Jacksons and (Billy) Cross & Fred Gerard scattered with my Indians across the whole front and I did not believe the report. After discussion Lt. (Luther) Hare was ordered to report to me as an assistant and I changed horses and went back the ten miles with some of my Rees and found where quite a party had gone up a stream with their travois to find a suitable crossing and . . . had worked back to the main trail." (11)

The implication seems to have been, at least in Custer's mind, that the Arikaras were not eager to meet the Lakota in battle. He sensed the drop in morale. But when Varnum, having been stung by Custer's criticism, returned from his next reconnaissance he said that the Crow scouts, the big men who knew the country, had pointed out a peak to be known as the Crow's Nest where they could actually see the Lakota village ahead.

Custer conferred with the Arikaras. "What do you think of this report of the Crow scouts?" Custer asked. "They say there are large camps of the Sioux. What do you suppose will be the outcome of it all?" (12)

Stabbed, one of the leading scouts, started to hop around the campfire pretending to dodge bullets in a sort of war dance.

"Chief, this is part of our tactics; when we dodge around like this we make it hard for the enemy to hit us," Stabbed told Custer. "We have learned from the Sioux that they have shot you whites down like buffalo calves. You stand in rows, erect, and do not dodge about, so it is easy to shoot you."

"I don't doubt you, Stabbed," Custer replied through Frederic Gerard. "What you say seems reasonable. I know you people, you are tricky like the coyote, you know how to hide, to creep up and take by surprise."

The other officers gathered around the scouts and Custer told Gerard that he wanted the Arikara to go into battle to take the horses from the Sioux, not to fight in line like the cavalry troopers.

"Some of you I see here have been with me on one or two other expeditions, and to see you again makes my heart glad," Custer told the scouts. "And on this expedition if we are victorious, when we return home, Bloody Knife, Bob-tailed Bull, Soldier, Strikes Two and Stabbed will be proud to have following behind them on parade marches those who have shown themselves to be brave young men. When your chief, Son-of-the-Star sees you on parade, I am sure he will be proud of his boys."

He told Gerard to tell the Arikara scouts once again that they could always expect his help: "I want you to tell these young men, these boys, that if we are successful, when we return, my brother, Bloody Knife, and I will represent you in Washington and perhaps we will take you in person to Washington." (13)

On the morning of June 25, Custer then rode to the Crow's Nest personally with some of the Crow and Arikara scouts and peered off toward where the scouts were pointing. Varnum and Custer both had trouble seeing the Indians but the Crows said that Sioux scouts had already seen them. Custer finally accepted that the scouts had found the Sioux camp but doubted that the command had been seen.

"I say again we have not been seen," Custer reportedly told the Crow and Arikara scouts. "That camp has not seen us. I am going ahead to carry out what I think. I will wait until it is dark and then we will march, we will place our army around the Sioux camp." (14)

"That plan is bad, it should not be carried out," said Big Belly, one of the Crows. The other Crows muttered agreement.

"Well, General. If you don't find more Indians in that valley than you ever saw together you can hang me," said Mitch Boyer, a French-Sioux interpreter for the Crows.

"It would do a damn sight of good to hang you, wouldn't it?" Custer said sarcastically. Varnum was surprised to hear Custer say "damn" because Custer seldom used any profane language whatsoever. (15)

Some of the Arikaras agreed with the Crows. They also thought the camp behind them had been spotted due to campfires. When Custer and Varnum were returning to camp, Varnum assumed Custer had decided to wait for nightfall. But Custer learned that a sergeant who had gone back to search for a box of hardtack had found Indians rifling the box, and had shot a Lakota teenager. Custer changed his mind. He would attack immediately to achieve surprise.

(1)   Libby, Orin, THE ARIKARA NARRATIVE. This is the last time THE ARIKARA NARRATIVE mentions Left Hand by that name during his lifetime. The Arikara narrators continue to note four Lakota scouts under the same names that Red Star mentioned in describing the parade at Fort Abraham Lincoln: Cards, or Caroo; Mathó-ská, or White Bear; Maȟpíya-ská or White Cloud, and Pté-até, or Buffalo Ancestor.

(2)   Ibid, Page 70, Page 139 for Running Wolf's different list of names.

(3)   Ibid, Page 70

(4)   Ibid, Page 70

(5)   Custer, Elizabeth, BOOTS AND SADDLES, Page 311)

(6)   Libby, Orin, THE ARIKARA NARRATIVE, Page 75-76

(7)   Custer, Elizabeth, BOOTS AND SADDLES, Page 312.

(8)   Graham. THE CUSTER MYTH, Page 130, Godfrey's account.

(9)   Libby, Orin, THE ARIKARA NARRATIVE, Page 78

10)   Ibid, Page 79

11)   Camp, Walter Mason, CUSTER IN '76, Pages 59-60 note

12)   Ibid, Pages 81-82

13)   Ibid, Page 82

14)   Libby, THE ARIKARA NARRATIVE, Page 92

15)   Camp. Walter Mason, CUSTER IN '76, Notes on Page 61.

INTO THE VALLEY OF DEATH

The Pȟaláni [Arikara] scouts and the four Lakȟóta scouts saw Custer's command party coming and expected battle. The younger men grouped themselves around the older men, as was their custom when getting ready for a big fight.

Custer rode up and said through Frederic Gerard, the white man with the blue eyes and the big beard: "Boys, I want you to take the horses away from the Sioux camp. . . . Make up your minds to go straight to their camp and capture their horses. Boys, you are going to have a hard day. You must keep up your courage, you will get experience today." (1)

The bugle sounded and Gerard told the scouts to charge. The P̌haláni scouts war-whooped and thundered past a Lakȟóta burial thípi [tipi]. Two Strikes struck the thípi with his whip and Young Hawk dismounted, slit the side of the thípi with his belt knife, and saw a wrapped body on a scaffold. He slipped back on his horse and raced ahead. The P̌haláni scouts with good horses were catching up to the soldiers ahead of them. The scouts with the best horses were soon in the lead, with the soldiers in the middle and scouts with bad horses left farther behind. Young Hawk rode through a dry coulee and a prairie dog town and saw the Little Big Horn River on his left. Red Star, Goose, Boy Chief and Red Bear were already across the river.

Young Hawk expected to be killed and scalped so he stopped his horse, unbraided his long hair and tied on a cluster of eagle feathers, and brushed his hair forward. He looked up and saw to his surprise that the white soldiers were forming a skirmish line instead of crossing into the Lakȟóta camp. The Lakȟóta were milling around fighting from the far side of the river.

Bob-tailed Bull, the war chief of the P̌haláni scouts, took a position on the far left of the skirmish line and Red Bear, Little Brave, Young Hawk's father

Forked Horn, Red Foolish Bear, Goose, and two Crows lined up facing the Lakȟóta and started shooting.

Bloody Knife rode up and called out to Young Hawk: "What Custer has ordered about the Sioux Horses is being done, the Sioux horses are being taken away." (2)

Some of the soldiers in the skirmish line were hit, and the Lakȟóta were fighting in greater numbers. One Lakȟóta charged the soldiers and was killed, but his sorrel horse broke through and Young Hawk caught it. Big Belly needed a horse, because his own horse was failing him, so Young Hawk gave it to him.

Suddenly a swarm of Lakȟóta on horseback exploded over a ridge and rode down on the skirmish line from the left. Bob-tailed Bull was driven back but he fell back still shooting, with his face to the enemy. A friendly soldier near Young Hawk shouted: "John, you go!" in English. Young Hawk and the friendly soldier ran for the timber near the river. So did everybody else. (3)

Young Hawk heard his father Forked Horn call out: "Let's go off and make a stand." (4)

Young Hawk and Goose made it across the river, following the soldiers. Goose was shot and cried out: "Cousin, I am wounded."

"When I heard this my heart did not tremble with fear but I made up my mind that I would die," Young Hawk remembered years later. (5) A Lakȟóta bullet dropped Goose's horse but Young Hawk drew Goose clear and sat him up against a tree. Goose was badly shot in the right hand. He told Goose to hold his horse. Goose had lost his rifle but still had a revolver in his belt. Young Hawk saw Big Belly—the same man who told Custer his plan was not good—crawling toward him through the brush.

"My friend is being killed, he is just on the edge of the thicket," Big Belly said. Young Hawk helped Big Belly—also known as Half-Yellow-Face—drag his friend White Swan back to the same tree where Goose was sitting.

"The sight of the wounded men gave me queer feelings. I did not want to see them mutilated, so I decided to get killed myself at the edge of the timber," Young Hawk said later. Before going out I put my arms around my horse's neck, saying 'I love you.' I then crawled out and stood up and saw all in front of me Sioux warriors kneeling ready to shoot. I fired at them and received a volley, but was not hit. I was determined to try again and get killed, so I crawled out to the edge of the timber in a new place, jumped up and fired again and received a volley, but I dropped out of sight before I was hit. Then I saw near me a tree with drift-wood piled against it, making a very good protection, and behind it I found Forked Horn lying face down to avoid being shot." (6)

Young Hawk's father Forked Horn scolded him for making himself a target: "Don't you do so again, it is no way to act. This is not the way to fight at all, to show yourself as a mark." (7)

Young Hawk, listening to his father, fell back on shooting from concealment and reported that he killed two Lakȟóta warriors and a horse. He heard the Lakȟóta women singing the tremolo to encourage their warriors. Some of the Pȟaláni tried to shoot the women, but missed. The firing let up, and late in the day Young Hawk saw an American flag from what was now Reno Hill, the bastion where Marcus Reno had led the men of his three companies and some of the scouts who had fled the timber in terror and confusion.

Young Hawk, Forked Horn and Half Yellow Face got Goose and White Swan onto their horses and made a dash for the hill with Young Hawk waving a white flag on a stick. The solders on the hill and the Lakȟóta and Šahíyela [Cheyenne] around the base of the hill both opened fire. The horse Young Hawk said he loved was hit and killed, but the scouts themselves survived unscathed.

Captain Frederick Benteen's three companies, and the mule pack train under Captain Thomas Mc-Dougall had also reached Reno Hill. The soldiers of the seven surviving companies were digging in with knives and tin cups and plates. Lieutenant Varnum was there as well, and told Young Hawk in sign language that Bob-tailed Bull had been killed.

Bloody Knife had also been killed. After rounding up some of the Lakȟóta horses, Bloody Knife had joined Major Reno after Reno retreated back into the timber along the banks of the Little Big Horn. Reno asked Bloody Knife for advice. As Bloody Knife leaned toward Reno to try to understand what Reno was asking, a Lakȟóta had slipped into the timber. His bullet shattered Bloody Knife's head and sprayed Reno with brains and blood. A Bad Talker soldier man, a German, was hit and wounded in the same volley. Three other soldiers tried to get him on his horse but he knew he was dying and told them "Leave me alone, for God's sake." (8)

Reno shouted for a retreat and led his soldiers across the Little Big Horn with the angry Indians mingling in among them or firing as they ran. (9) Some of the officers thought that Reno was a coward, but some of the enlisted men said that if they had not been commanded by a coward there would have been no survivors on Reno Hill.

Strikes Two, another Pȟaláni scout, had actually forded the Little Big Horn with the Lakȟóta scouts Caroo—also known as Bear Running In The Timber—Watȟó-ská, (Matȟó-ská, or White Bear, and Maȟpíya-ská, White Cloud). Strikes Two reported that his party stole a number of Lakȟóta horses as Custer had ordered. Bob-tailed Bull told them to look for a way to escape if the soldiers retreated "as there are more people here than we thought." (10) Strikes Two mentioned that three of Custer's Sioux scouts, Watȟó-ská (Matȟó-ská[?], White Cloud, and Caroo joined his group of Pȟaláni scouts when they broke out and rode for the Rosebud. Soldier, another scout, reported that Maȟpíya-ská (White Cloud) caught a black Sioux horse just before they reached the Rosebud. The black Lakȟóta horse was clever and sniffed the ground to try to find his own trail back to the village—but the scouts were not headed back for the Lakȟóta village.

Young Hawk stayed on Reno Hill with the seven surviving companies until the Lakȟóta and Šahíyela [Cheyenne] left the field two days later as General Terry arrived with the Gatling guns and the other troops on June 27. The scouts were among the first to search the battlefield for the bodies of friends and to help recover the bodies of the soldiers.

"The body of Bloody Knife lay a little back from the brush near the ford," Young Hawk remembered years later. . . . The five thípis [tipis] in the deserted Dakȟóta camp were thrown down and some of the bodies stripped by the soldiers they had seen there. They went on to the Dakȟóta [Lakȟóta] camp and found the body of a dead Dakȟóta lying on a tanned buffalo hide. Young Hawk recognized this warrior as one who had been a scout at Fort Lincoln, Čhatká. He had on a white shirt, the shoulders were painted green, and on his forehead, painted in red, was the sign of a secret society." (11)

Left Hand—Napé Čhatká in Lakȟóta—had come back to his people and had been given an honorable burial.

(1)   Libby, Orin, THE ARIKARA NARRATIVE, Page 93

(2)   Ibid, Page 96

(3)   Ibid, Page 97

(4)   Ibid, Page 97

(5)   Ibid, Page 99

(6)   Ibid, Page 100

(7)   Ibid, Page 100

(8)   Find-A-Grave, Henry Klotzbucher, born in the German state of Baden in 1848. Indians referred to Germans as Bad Talkers because they recognized that German was a language similar to English, but that Germans did not seem to speak English well..

(9)   Camp, Walter Mason, CUSTER IN '76, Page 223. See also, Taylor, William O. WITH CUSTER ON THE LITTLE BIGHORN, Pages 35 - 55 for an intelligent enlisted man's first-hand account. I FOUGHT WITH CUSTER by the German-American Charles Windolph is also excellent.

(10)   Ibid, Notes on Page 184-185 and 190

(11)   Libby, THE ARIKARA NARRATIVE, Page 109

THE ENIGMA

The fact that Left Hand came back to his people after serving as an Army scout and died fighting at the Little Bighorn is documented. The Standing Rock Sioux Reservation, the home of the Hunkpapa Lakota today, carries his Lakota name in the list of those who fought in 1876, using the Lakota version of his name, Čhatká, which means Left (Hand):

"Chat-ka. Hunkpapa Sioux. His body was found in abandoned tipi in the valley, after the Little Bighorn Battle. He was a scout at Fort Lincoln."

There is no question that Left Hand had been a scout for Custer and was later found laid out with honors by the Hunkpapa. The only question is—when did he come back to his tribe?

When Custer reached a vantage point overlooking the Lakota and Cheyenne villages he had said he would attack the Indians while the Arikara [Pȟaláni] and Lakota scouts rode with Major Reno to enclose the opposite side. He must have been startled at the size of the encampment. But he must also have thought that "Custer's Luck" was still with him.

The last white man known to have seen Custer alive was the Italian-born Trumpeter Giovanni Martini, sometimes known as John Martin. Walter Mason Camp interviewed Martini on October 24, 1908.

". . . Custer halted command on the high ridge about 10 minutes, and officers looked at the village through glasses," Camp recorded, paraphrasing Martini. "Saw children and dogs playing among the tepees but no warriors or horses except a few loose ponies grazing around. There was then a discussion among the officers as to where the warriors might be and someone suggested that they might be buffalo hunting, recalling that they had seen skinned buffalo along the trail on June 24.

"Custer now made a speech to his men saying, 'We will go down and make a crossing and capture the village.' The whole command then pulled off their hats and cheered. And the consensus of opinion seemed to be among the officers that if this could be done the Indians would have to surrender when they would return, in order not to fire on their women and children." (1)

Martini told Camp that he had ridden about a half-mile toward the villages when Custer's adjutant, Canadian-born First Lieutenant W.W. Cooke, handed him a note and told him to find Senior Captain Frederick Benteen, who had been sent to scout off to the left with three companies. Martini accepted the note: "Benteen. Come On. Big Village. Bring Packs. PS. Bring Packs. W.W. Cooke" (2)

On the way to find Benteen, Martini met Boston Custer, the general's younger brother, and told him which way Custer had gone. Boston followed George and Tom Custer, their nephew Autie Reed, and their brother-in-law Lieutenant James Calhoun toward the villages while Martini rode the other way to find Benteen.

"When Martin got to top of ridge he looked down in village and saw Indians charging like swarm of bees toward the ford, waving buffalo hides (to frighten the horses)," Camp recorded. "At the same time he saw Custer retreating up the open county in the direction of the battlefield . . . The Indians were firing straggling shots. About this time Martin was fired on by Indians in the bluffs between him and river and they hit his horse on hip and blood spattered on Martin's back." (3)

Martin reached Captain Benteen and gave him the message. Accounts differ as to how well Martin explained Custer's situation at the time. As Captain Benteen rode toward the growing sounds of the gunfire he saw the Indians chasing Reno's command and the Arikara scouts across the Little Big Horn and up Reno Hill. Benteen joined Reno and essentially took over command of the Reno Hill contingent. They were shortly joined by the soldiers and teamsters with the mule pack train and fugitive scouts and soldiers from the valley fight that ended in Reno's rout. More of the 7th Cavalry and many of the Indian scouts were now concentrated on Reno Hill. Most of them—51 per cent of the entire Seventh Cavalry—survived two days of sniping, thirst, and terror.

The five companies that had followed Custer from the opposite side were wiped out by overwhelming Indian gunfire. Custer, who desperately needed a victory as he had told the scouts, has apparently lapsed into wishful thinking. He looked down at the village and saw only women, children, and dogs—and thought that the men were off hunting buffalo. In fact, the men and teenaged boys were sleeping off a tribal dance that had gone on for the entire night before (4), and they were sleeping next to their rifles—often repeating rifles or the surplus infantry rifles Elizabeth Custer had seen being shipped to the trading posts. The result of the unexpected barrage of gunfire, most of it from repeating rifles, was devastating.

"We were better armed than the Long Swords," (5) said Rain-In-The-Face, a leading warrior and unrepentant killer of troopers. "Their guns wouldn't shoot but once—the thing [ejector] wouldn't throw out the empty cartridge shells . . . When we found out they could not shoot we saved our bullets by knocking the long swords over with our war clubs—it was just like killing sheep. Some of them got on their knees and begged; we spared none—ugh! . . . one long sword escaped though; his pony ran off with him and went past our lodges. They told me about it in Chicago. I saw the man there, and I remembered hearing the squaws tell about it after the fight."

The man who escaped was Sergeant August Finckle of C Company, originally Frank Finkle, an Ohio farm boy who had joined the Army in January of 1872 in Chicago and given his birthplace as "Berlin, Prussia" in American handwriting. Finckle turned up in Dayton, Washington, a few years after the battle, still spelling his name "Finckle" in the same American handwriting until it slowly turned into "Finkle" and later "Finkel" on deeds and legal papers including the probate of his first wife's last will and testament in 1921 and his own last will and testament in 1930.

Finkel had the same incongruous six-foot-plus height—the official limit in the cavalry was five-foot-10—and the same dark hair color, pale eye color, and handwriting as "August Finckle." Both men spoke German—and both reportedly spoke it rather badly. When a tintype of August Finckle turned up in the 21st Century, August Finckle and Frank Finkel turned out to have exactly the same face, with allowances for age. Finkel's case is still "controversial" to those who want the Little Bighorn to be an American Thermopylae.

The reality is that while Custer's five companies lost "about" 210 men, the official body count on the field varied between 197 and 206. Private Nathan Short was found dead and caught under his dead horse about 25 miles from the battlefield, and a skull and skeleton plausibly identified as Lieutenant Henry Moore Harrington was found some miles from the field in the same northeastern direction as that yielded Short's body and what was probably Finckle's dead horse. A sorrel C Company horse had made it all the way to the confluence of the Rosebud and the Yellowstone before it was shot once in the head and abandoned. (6)

The battle known as Custer's Last Stand was a debacle. Custer and his brothers and some of the other officers and sergeants appear to have put up a great fight on what became known as Custer Hill, but about 40 enlisted men broke and ran, and were killed downhill in the Deep Ravine, and these, rather than Custer, were almost certainly the last men to die. The 7th Cavalry lost 268 officers and men, sustained 58 wounded.

A number of officers and men understandably suffered nervous breakdowns and died of acute alcoholism within the next few years. Major Reno, who panicked when Bloody Knife's blood and brains were blown into his face, and Captain Benteen, who won the Medal of Honor saving Reno Hill, both drank their way out of the Army after disgraceful episodes involving drunken brawls and, in Reno's case, a bungled bid at adultery with a brother officer's wife and a Peeping Tom incident. (7)

The Indians lost about 26 warriors, possibly as many as 32. Rain-In-The-Face told W. Kent Thomas "about ten and four or ten and six" but he was speaking only of Lakota dead. Gall, the war chief for the

Hunkpapas, told reporters that only 43 Indians were killed: "My two squaws and three children were killed there by the pale-faced warriors, and it made my heart bad. After that, I killed all my enemies with the hatchet." (8) The death toll of Indian women and children is generally given as 10 to 16.

White Bull, a prominent member of the Northern Cheyenne tribe, listed 26 warriors killed in the Custer fight, including 19 Lakota and seven Cheyenne. (8) White Bull lists Čhatká (Left Hand) as a Cheyenne killed in the Custer Fight. His list of Cheyenne killed gives them Lakota names. But the Northern Cheyenne were affiliated with the Lakota and sometimes spoke Lakota, an easier language, even among themselves. The Southern Cheyenne sometimes dryly dubbed the Northern Cheyenne "Ho'óhomō'e"—"The Sioux."

Notably, the Cheyenne concealed their dead in the earth while the Lakota exposed them to the sky, which means that Indian bodies seen after the battle were only Lakota. (9) Major Marcus Reno, in his official report of July 5, 1876, said he saw 18 Indian bodies but assumed that many more had been killed. Reno's visual tally of the Lakota dead matches the Lakota warrior death counts of Rain-In-The-Face, Gall, and White Bull rather closely. But Reno was more concerned about the white death count.

"The harrowing sight of the dead bodies crowning the height on which Custer fell, and which will remain vividly in my memory until death, is too recent for me not to ask the good people of this country whether a policy that sets the opposing parties in the field, armed, clothed and equipped by one and the same Government, should not be abolished," Reno wrote in his official report of the battle. (10) This was probably the best thing Reno ever said to explain the catastrophe of 268 U.S. soldiers killed for a loss of 26 to 32 Indian warriors.

When a hearing was convened at the Palmer House Hotel in Chicago in January of 1879, Captain Frederick Benteen spoke to reporters outside the hearing where Reno was cleared of rumored cowardice in what some critics said was a whitewash. Benteen blamed the whole thing on the Indian Department.

"For the past twelve or fifteen years I think the Indian Bureau has been entirely responsible, and the cause has been the enormous pilfering and stealing from the Indians. . . . their acts have created dissatisfaction among the savages which they have been unable to suppress. No agent can save $13,000 or $15,000 annually legitimately out of a salary of $1,500, and yet numbers of them do it. . . . If [the Indians] were treated more considerately and received what the government allows them, I think there is no doubt they would be perfectly peaceful and tractable. It is this constant robbery which goads them to outbreaks. . . . We should treat the Indian as if he possesses some natural feeling. If that were done and the other reforms carried out, the Indian would soon cease troubling us, and more cheerfully give himself up to the processes of civilization." (11)

Custer and Left Hand both died, in the end, because of the corruption that left Major Marcus Reno and Captain Frederick Benteen and the Lakota and Cheyenne as the scapegoats of the "Custer Massacre." Custer himself had denounced the corruption of the War Department and the Indian Bureau, so much so that his job was in jeopardy and he took one risk too many trying to win back the glory he had enjoyed as "The Boy General" during the Civil War, where he had helped save the Union at the Battle of Gettysburg. Left Hand—like Custer—wanted to feed his family. But Left Hand was unable, in the end, to turn against his own people, and they took him back and gave him an honorable funeral.

But when did Left Hand actually leave the 7th Cavalry scouts, and how did he die?

Left Hand's name disappears from the Arikara Narrative of the other scouts after his return from the mail run to Fort Lincoln before and after the snow-storm in the first week of June 1. Another name disap-pears from the Arikara Narrative after the battle— Pté-até, Buffalo Ancestor. A Sioux named The Whole Buffalo is mentioned during the horse-stealing that was an early part of the battle, and then he disappears as well. (12) The other three Lakota scouts are consistently mentioned through the remainder of the expedition.

Left Hand has living relatives among the Hunk-papa people of the Standing Rock Sioux Reservation. They acknowledge that he was killed at the Little Big-horn and laid out for an honorable burial by his people, as the tribal history says. But they have no further knowledge of when Left Hand left the soldiers and joined the Lakota and Cheyenne, or how he died.

One curious legend, however, was recorded by Colonel Albert B. Welch, a friend of the Hunkpapa La-kota people and long-term resident of Mandan, North Dakota near the Standing Rock Sioux Reservation. Co-lonel Welch, the son of the Methodist minister from Iowa who later lived in Washington state, was born two years before the Little Bighorn and died in 1945. He served in the Philippine Insurrection, the Mexican Border incident, and the Meuse-Argonne offensive of 1918 in France during World War I—the bloodiest battle in American history. He deplored the Philippine

Insurrection, and World War I seems to have convinced him that war was not in any way glorious.

Welch always prided himself on his friendship to the Sioux. In in 1913 he was named as the adopted son of Chief John Grass, also known as Charging Bear. who was famous as a young man for his rescue of the white captive, Fanny Kelly, and as an older man for negotiating peaceful relations between Indians and whites.

In 1922, Colonel Welch recorded a story by Emeron White, an educated Hunkpapa, as a legend of the Little Bighorn.

"The Sioux people sing a song about a Ree scout who died with Custer," Emeron White told Colonel Welch. "They call him Maȟpíya Ťhatȟáŋka (Buffalo Cloud). He rode a swift horse but it was wounded and they got around him. The scout begged for his life and named the first born of the families of those Húŋkpapȟa who were around him. This is sacred to the people to name the first born and they always let an enemy get away when they do that. But this time everybody was excited and so they killed him there. I think maybe it was Bloody Knife, his other name. They are all sorry for that now and sing this song in his honor:

"The horse came alone
Where is his rider?
Where is Buffalo Cloud?
Here he lays." (13)

Through the haze of time, the man who was killed was not Bloody Knife, because Bloody Knife was killed near the Little Bighorn river in the timber while speaking to Major Reno. Nobody among the Hunkpapa felt sorry about his death except for his sister, who recognized his battered head when her two daughters brought it into camp, amputated, beaten to a pulp and scalped. (14) Young Hawk later identified Bloody's Knife's separated scalp by a streak of grey hair among the black. (15) The Hunkpapa hated Bloody Knife because—not without considerable reason—he had taken sides with the white soldiers and the Arikaras against his father's people. Bloody Knife's death was not mourned but celebrated. The Sioux left his head behind in a bucket as a gift or warning to the soldiers.

The Arikara lost three warriors at the Little Bighorn—Bloody Knife, Bob-tailed Bull, and Little Brave, whose body was never found, though Young Hawk found his horse. Goose, Young Hawk's cousin, was wounded in the hand but recovered. Was the "Ree" whose death Emeron White described to Colonel Welch the missing Little Brave—or was he Left Hand?

Emeron White called the "Ree" Maȟpíya Tȟatȟáŋka, Buffalo Cloud. The Lakota scout who disappears from the Arikara Narrative in the aftermath of the Little Bighorn was Pté-até, Buffalo Ancestor, literally "Buffalo Cow Father." Both names contain the buffalo as an element: Tȟatȟáŋka refers to a bull buffalo and Pté to buffalo in general or to the more edible cow buffalo. The Lakota language is rich in buffalo names. The "Ree" who was killed by the Hunkpara Lakota had a very fast horse. The horse owned by Pté-até was chosen as the champion by the Lakota scouts in the horse race against the Arikara, Stabbed (the race occurred after the column left Fort Abraham Lincoln on the march that ended at the Little Bighorn). (16)

Most startling of all, the trapped scout was able to list all the first-born children of those Hunkpapas who surrounded him—presumably in the Lakota language, not in Arikara. Lakota was widely spoken by other tribes. But being able to recognize the faces of enemy Indians and recall the names of their first-born children argues strongly that the scout was one of their own.

Perhaps Left Hand came back to his people a day or two after he returned with the mail, two weeks before the battle of the Little Bighorn. Sitting Bull famously had a vision of soldiers falling into camp upside down and heard a voice saying "I give you these because they have no ears." People who are skeptical about the supernatural could argue that Left Hand may have made his way to Sitting Bull's tipi more than a week before the battle and warned him that Custer was coming. Against this argument, Custer actually achieved complete tactical surprise, just as he thought he had: while the "hostile" Lakota knew they were at war with the United States, the attack on June 25 surprised them just as Custer had expected. Custer's surprise—his last—came because the Lakota and Cheyenne were so heavily armed with repeating rifles, and because the warriors and teenagers were sleeping in the tipis in the afternoon and not off somewhere hunting buffalo.

Left Hand may have brought an early warning, but if he did, it did no good. He may also have changed his mind only when he actually started out in an attack on his own people and tried to change sides at the last minute. Dubiously, he may not have changed sides at all, though his own people would not have given him an honored rest with ceremonial honors if they thought he was a traitor. He would have been given the same treatment as Bloody Knife. Instead, the Hunkpapa Lakota sang songs of sadness about a young warrior they may have killed by mistake. Left Hand, who sang his death song about dying surrounded by enemies when he rode out with the scouts from Fort Abraham Lincoln, may have tragically died surrounded by friends who only thought Left Hand was an enemy.

(1)   Camp, Walter Mason, CUSTER IN '76, Page 100

(2)   Graham, W.A, "THE CUSTER MYTH, Page 299, photograph of actual note.

(3)   Camp, Walter Mason, CUSTER IN '76, Page 101

(4)   Marquis, Thomas B., MD, WOODEN LEG: A WARRIOR WHO FOUGHT CUSTER, Page Pages 215 -216 and Neihardt, John G., BLACK ELK SPEAKS, Page 108. The dance is also mentioned by Mildred Fielder but not in many other accounts and is ignored by military historians and proponents of a "Sioux Ambush."

(5)   Brady, Cyrus Townsend, INDIAN FIGHTS AND FIGHTERS, Pages 285 and 291, from an interview published in 1904 by W. Kent Thomas. "Long Sword" is Míla-háŋskA, Long Knife, the Lakota name for a cavalryman. The name is generic and troopers did not carry sabers at the Little Bighorn. The forensic archaeology described in ARCHAELOGY, HISTORY AND CUSTER'S LAST STAND by Richard Allan Fox confirms the first-hand personal account by Rain-In-The-Face is substantially accurate.

(6)   Graham, THE CUSTER MYTH, Page 146 and Brininstool, E.A., TROOPERS WITH CUSTER, Pages 246—248, the original and the expanded accounts of General Edward S. Godfrey, a Little Bighorn survivor with Reno and later winner of the Medal of Honor.

(7) Connell, Evan S. SON OF THE MORNING STAR, Pages 28 to 62 discusses the immensely sad self-destruction of the two ranking officers after General Custer. The fact that Frederick Benteen and, more especially, Marcus Reno, were both blamed for the Custer catastrophe can only have contributed to their personality disorders. Several officers who no command responsibility enjoyed successful careers in the Army were later promoted and retired voluntarily many years later.

(8) Graham, W.A., THE CUSTER MYTH, Pages 89—90

(9) Camp, Walter Mason, CUSTER IN '76, Page 267

(10) Reno, Marcus A., REPORT OF M.A. RENO. Concluding paragraph

(11) Graham, W.A., THE CUSTER MYTH, Page 214, taken from the *Chicago Times* of January 25, 1879

(12) Camp, Walter Mason, CUSTER IN '76, Page 184

(13) Welch, Albert B. ORAL HISTORY OF THE DAKOTA TRIBES, under Emeron White.

(14) Connell, Evan S. SON OF THE MORNING STAR, Page 15

(15) Libby, Orin, THE ARIKARA NARRATIVE. Page 111

(16) Ibid, Page 66

BIBLIOGRAPHY

Barnett, Louise, TOUCHED BY FIRE: THE LIFE, DEATH, AND MYTHIC AFTERLIFE OF GEORGE ARMSTRONG CUSTER, Henry Holt, New York, 1996

Brady, Cyrus Townsend, INDIAN FIGHTS AND FIGHTERS. University of Nebraska Press, Lincoln, 1971 reprint, original publication 1904, account, taken from W. Kent Thomas, "The Personal Story of Rain-in-the-Face," as written down in 1894.

Brininstool, E.A., TROOPERS WITH CUSTER, Stackpole Books, Mechanicsburg, Pennsylvania, 1954

Brown, Dee, BURY MY HEART AT WOUNDED KNEE: AN INDIAN HISTORY OF THE AMERICAN WEST, Henry Holt and Company, 1970.

Brown, Joseph Epes, THE SACRED PIPE: BLACK ELK'S ACCOUNT OF THE SEVEN RITUALS OF THE SIOUX, Penguin Books, Baltimore, Maryland, 1971

Camp, Walter Mason, CUSTER IN '76, edited by Kenneth Hammer, Brigham Young University, Provo, Utah, 1976

Clark, Robert A., THE KILLING OF CHIEF CRAZY HORSE, Bison Books, University of Nebraska Press, Lincoln and London, 1988 (reprint of 1977 Arthur H. Clark Edition)

Custer, Elizabeth, BOOTS AND SADDLES, OR LIFE IN THE DAKOTAS WITH GENERAL CUSTER, Harper & Brothers, New York, 1885 (facsimile edition)

Fielder, Mildred, SIOUX INDIAN LEADERS, Crown Publishers, New York, 1975

Fox, Richard Allan Fox, ARCHAEOLOGY, HISTORY, AND CUSTER'S LAST BATTLE, University of Oklahoma Press, Norman and London, 1997

Graham, W.A. THE CUSTER MYTH, A SOURCE BOOK OF CUSTERIANA, Stackpole Books, Mechanicsburg, Pennsylvania, 1953

Kelly, Fanny NARRATIVE OF MY CAPTIVITY AMONG THE SIOUX INDIANS, Konecky & Konecky, New York, 1990 (reprint, with notes, of 1864 edition)

Koster, John, CUSTER SURVIVOR: THE END OF A MYTH, THE BEGINNING OF A LEGEND, History Publishing, Palisades, New York 2010

Libby, Orin G, THE ARIKARA NARRATIVE OF CUSTER's CAMPAIGN AND THE BATTLE OF THE LITTLE BIGHORN, University of Oklahoma Press, Norman, Oklahoma, 1998 (reprint of 1920 edition, The Arikara Narrative of the Campaign Against the Hostile Dakotas, 1876

Maddow, Ben, A SUNDAY BETWEEN WARS: THE COURSE OF AMERICAN LIFE FROM 1865 TO 1917, W.W. Norton & Company, 1979

Marquis, Thomas B., MD, WOODEN LEG, A WARRIOR WHO FOUGHT CUSTER, Bison Books, University of Nebraska Press, reprint of 1931 edition by Midwest Books.

Marquis, Thomas B., MD, KEEP THE LAST BULLET FOR YOURSELF: THE TRUE STORY OF CUSTER'S LAST STAND, Reference Publications, New York, 1976

McFeeley, William S., GRANT: A BIOGRAPHY, W.W. Norton & Company, New York and London, 1981

Nadeau, Remi, FORT LARAMIE AND THE SIOUX, Crest Publishers, Santa Barbara, California, 1997 (revised version of FORT LARAMIE AND THE SIOUX INDIANS. Prentice-Hall, Englewood Cliffs, New Jersey, 1967

Parkman, Francis, THE OREGON TRAIL, reprinted for members of the Heritage Club, Norwalk, Connecticut, 1943, 1971. First published in 1847 in Knickerbockers Magazine form, book published 1849 by G.P. Putnam.

Reedstrom, Ernest Lisle, BUGLES, BANNERS, AND WAR BONNETS, Bonanza Books, New York, 1986 (Reprint of Caxton Publishers, Caldwell, Idaho, 1977

Smith, Jean Edward, GRANT, Simon and Schuster, New York, 2001

Taylor, William O., WITH CUSTER ON THE LITTLE BIGHORN, Viking Penguin Books, New York, 1996

Utley, Robert. M., CAVALIER IN BUCKSKIN: GEORGE ARMSTRONG CUSTER AND THE WESTERN MILITARY FRONTIER, University of Oklahoma Press, Norman and London, 1988

Wallace, David Rains, THE BONEHUNTERS' REVENGE: DINOSAURS, GREED, AND THE GREATEST SCIENTIFIC FEUD OF THE GILDED AGE, Houghton Mifflin Company, Boston, 1999

Windolph, Charles, I FOUGHT WITH CUSTER: THE STORY OF SERGEANT WINDOLPH, as told to Frazier and Robert Hunt, Charles Scribner's Sons, New York, 1947

TROOPER AND BRAVE: MILITARY AFFAIRS IN THE TRANS-MISSISSIPPI WEST, National Park Service, published by Harper & Row, Publishers, New York, Evanston, and London, 1963

PROCEEDINGS OF THE SENATE SITTING FOR THE TRIAL OF WILLIAM W. BELKNAP, LATE SECRETARY OF WAR, ON THE ARTICLES OF IMPEACHMENT EXHIBITED BY THE HOUSE OF REPRESENTATIVES
Forty-Forth Congress, First Session, Washington, Government Printing Office, 1876 (rare book)

Reno, Marcus, REPORT OF M.A. RENO ON THE BATTLE OF THE LITTLE BIG HORN, JULY 5, 1876

ENCYCLOPEDIAS

AMERICAN NATIONAL BIOGRAPHY, Oxford
University Press, New York and London, 1999

DICTIONARY OF AMERICAN BIOGRAPHY,
Charles Scribner's Sons, New York, 1930
ENCYCLOPEDIA OF THE AMERICAN CIVIL
WAR: A POLITICAL, SOCIAL AND MILITARY
HISTORY, David Heidler and Jeanne Heidler, editors-
in-chief ABC-CLIO, Inc., Santa Barbara, California,
2000

SCHOLARLY PAPERS

MANDAN HISTORICAL SOCIETY, Mandan,
North Dakota, web site.

ORAL HISTORY OF THE DAKOTA TRIBES—
1800'S—1945, Albert B. Welch

NEWSPAPERS

The New York Times, Obituary of Hiester Clymer, June 13, 1884

MAGAZINES

National Geographic, "IN THE SHADOW OF WOUNDED KNEE" by Alexandra Fuller, June, 2012

WILD WEST magazine, article, THE BELKNAP SCANDAL: FULCRUM TO DISASTER, by John Koster, June 2010.

ABOUT THE AUTHOR

John Koster is the co-author of *The Road To Wounded Knee*, a best-seller which won the N.J. Sigma Delta Chi Award for Distinguished Public Service in 1974, and of *Custer Survivor*, which inspired a two-hour documentary on The History Channel. A volunteer Viet Nam-era veteran injured in training with U.S. Army Airborne in 1967, Koster writes regularly for *Wild West*, *Military History*, and *American History*. He has written for *American Heritage* and *National Geographic*. He is fluent and literate in French, German, Dutch, Italian, Spanish and rudimentary Lakota, the language of the Sioux. All five of his grandchildren are either part Cherokee or part Sioux.

www.ingramcontent.com/pod-product-compliance
Lightning Source LLC
LaVergne TN
LVHW051104080426
835508LV00019B/2063